ST JAMES THE GREAT, RADLEY

The Story of a Village Church

Contributors: Richard Dudding

Brian and Rita Ford

Felicity Henderson

Joyce Huddleston

Pam McKellen

Tony Rogerson

Christine Wootton

Editor: Joyce Huddleston

Radley
Oxfordshire
www.radleyhistoryclub.org.uk

First published 2016

ISBN 978-0-9568632-4-9

Printed and bound by

Parchments of Oxford
Printworks, Crescent Road, Oxford OX4 2PB

Email: print@parchmentuk.com   www.parchmentuk.com

Contents

Acknowledgements

The contributors and Radley History Club are very grateful for all the help, advice and information provided during the writing and production of this book. We would particularly like to thank:

- Revd Pam McKellen for all her help and encouragement, including the sharing of her considerable knowledge about the church;

- Stanley Baker, the archivist of Radley History Club, for all his help and particularly for his painstaking work in transcribing wills and other documents;

- all those interviewed as part of the Club's recording of oral history and specifically for this book;

- the staff at the Berkshire Record Office;

- all those who commented on the final draft, pointing out errors or making useful suggestions to improve the text, but particularly Stanley Baker and Tony Gillman;

- Tony Gillman and Felicity Henderson for their meticulous proof-reading;

- Richard Dudding for producing the various maps and plans;

- Edwin Dudding and Phil Henderson for their help with the design of the cover.

The front cover photograph is by John Huddleston. The back cover photographs are by Les Hemsworth, John Huddleston, Joyce Huddleston and Pam McKellen. The providers of the photographs in each chapter are named at the end of that chapter. We thank all of them.

Notes from the editor

Clergy nomenclature. This is explained in full in Chapter 5, but all incumbents of Radley Church are called a 'vicar' unless there is a good reason to use a different title.

Dates. In 1752 there was a change in the calendar as a result of which each year started on 1 January not 24 March (Lady Day) as before. Where a date prior to 1752 falls between 1 January and 24 March, the year is given for both the old and the new calendar. For instance, the will of Sir William Stonhouse, 1st Baronet of Radley, is dated 20 January 1631 and so the year is given as 1631/2.

Family names. Spelling of family names varied greatly over the centuries and also between documents from the same era. For example, 'Sheen' might also appear as 'Sheene' or 'Shene'. If the authors have used different sources there may therefore appear to be inconsistencies between chapters in the spelling of the same family name.

'Old money'. Before decimalisation in 1971, the pound (£) was divided into 20 shillings (s), each of 12 pennies (d).

Web addresses. All web links given in the work were accessed in June 2016. We apologise if any of the links have since ceased to work.

Foreword

The moment you see the Church and Vicarage in Radley you realise that there is much more to explore. Walking into the Church and looking round, or browsing in the churchyard, raises questions and even a little knowledge leads us to desire to know more. The study of the history of the whole of the village and its surroundings has stimulated much interest and research by the members of Radley History Club, now focused on the Church. It is a pleasure to write the foreword to this book which explains so much about St James the Great Radley and its special part in the village.

Although there have been many changes in the village, the community and this parish over the centuries, the Church has always provided a centre of peace and refuge and a place for worship. Families have brought babies for baptism, lovers for weddings and loved ones for funerals. The Church's open door means that people can come in and sit, think and pray. Underpinning all the work and worship of the Church is a confidence in the basic, fundamental love of God for his people and a desire to share that love with all others.

In days of old the church was a place of sanctuary, a place where cattle may have been stored, villagers sheltered and all learnt the Lord's Prayer and Ten Commandments by rote. Everybody would be involved in their church in some way or another. Families and servants would march to church in their Sunday best. Children would be involved in the choir or in learning to ring the bells, and would learn their catechism as they prepared for confirmation. Today the children from Radley Primary School come into the Church to learn about the building, about weddings and baptisms, and other parts of the Christian faith. Sometimes they have Godly Play and other special celebrations including end of term services in the Church. To the children it is a familiar and comfortable place to be in.

Radley Church in 2016 is very different from the scene that people would have recognised 50 or even 20 years ago. The 2006 infestation by death watch beetle meant that the interior was transformed into a much more adaptable place than before. Now, pews and chairs can be moved, creating opportunities for all sorts of different uses; large spaces can be used for activities or exhibitions, and the chairs can be grouped for meetings or small informal services. Once again the Church is a versatile building that can be used by the whole community in many different ways.

The core of our worship has remained the same, with an emphasis on teaching the Bible and the basics of the Christian faith, combined with celebration of the Eucharist each week. Alongside the traditional forms of worship, new things have emerged: Iona services, all age worship, Messy Church and Reflect@6 (an evening service when we address a topical or ethical subject with an expert speaker). The variety of our worship is evident at major festivals like Christmas when one day the Church is filled with people feasting on mince pies and mulled wine after they have followed a lantern trail, discovering the Christmas story en route. Another day the walls are bursting with those who have come to the Crib service and then we fill the Church again for the Christmas Eve Communion service. Easter is different with quiet meditations during Holy Week, a very special 'hour at the Cross' on Good Friday and then celebrations on Easter Day beginning outside at 6 am round a fire!

We aim to be a welcoming place that is special to all the community and where each person can explore faith and find peace. We want people of all ages and stages to feel at home, so there are activities suitable for children, families and young people as well as a wide range of activities for people of all ages. Some of those who come to worship at the Church live outside the parish boundaries, but no distinction is made!

Life in the twenty-first century is very different from the olden days, but it has been encouraging to see that people in the village still identify with 'their' church and support its activities and appeals. It was exciting to see the way in which a wide range of people supported us when funds were needed to reorder the Church after the discovery of death watch beetle. More recently, many came into the Church for a special 'Bell' weekend to contribute when we needed to raise enough money in one weekend to repair some serious problems with the bells.

Originally one parish, Radley became a United Benefice with Sunningwell in October 1990 and, in January 2015, a new Benefice consisting of Radley, Sunningwell and Kennington was officially formed. The three churches now work together with the common aim of exploring together what Christian faith means in the twenty-first century and supporting each other in living in our communities as Jesus taught us to.

Revd Pam McKellen
Vicar of the Benefice of Radley, Sunningwell and Kennington

October 2016

Chapter 1: Introduction

by Joyce Huddleston

The Church of Saint James the Great is probably the oldest building in Radley, with the present building dating from the end of the thirteenth century. This book covers not only the exterior and interior of the Grade II* listed building, but also the burials in the churchyard, the clergy, the key roles played today by the laity, and the ways in which the Church has received money and helped others through charitable giving.

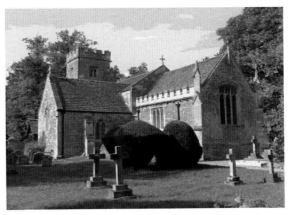

Radley Church from the south-east

About the book

The book is a collection of essays by various members of Radley History Club. Their research makes extensive use of the Club's archives but also draws on a range of other sources including recorded interviews with local people, online resources, books and directories, and records in regional and national archives. The research has corrected some facts, resulted in revised or new interpretations of previous beliefs, thrown light on some mysteries and evolved understanding of the past. The availability of new sources and better access to old ones has allowed us to review and extend what we know. However, historical facts can be elusive and new light may be shed in the future.

This chapter sets the scene by describing the village of Radley, the growth in its population over the years and the area covered today by the ecclesiastical parish of Radley. It also presents a short ecclesiastical history of the parish and an overview of three key players over the years – the Stonhouse and Bowyer families and latterly Radley College.

Chapter 2 by Richard Dudding describes the early origins, the building of the current church, the evolution of its structure over the centuries, and related buildings including the medieval, Grade II listed vicarage. In Chapter 3, Felicity Henderson provides a tour of the prominent features of the interior including the Norman font, pulpit canopy, reredos, memorials, bells and organ. Chapter 4 is a report by Brian and Rita Ford of their extensive study of the monuments and graves in the churchyard and the Lower Cemetery. In Chapter 5, Christine Wootton presents known facts and stories about the various clergy who have served Radley Church, going back to the first names recorded from the middle of the sixteenth century up to the present day. In Chapter 6, Richard Dudding tackles the important question of money – who has given the Church money and who has benefited from charitable giving by the Church. Chapter 7 by Pam McKellen and Tony Rogerson looks at the roles of the key people supporting the vicar in the day-to-day running of the Church today. The sources used are listed at the end of each chapter.

A timeline of the key events in the history of Radley Church is given in Appendix 1.

The book reflects the approach taken by the different authors to their topic and is not intended to be a comprehensive account of all aspects of Radley Church.

The village of Radley today

Radley lies on the River Thames to the north-east of the town of Abingdon-on-Thames and about five miles south of the city of Oxford. For centuries the village was part of north Berkshire, but moved into Oxfordshire in 1974 as part of the major alteration of county boundaries at that time. Local government services are provided by Oxfordshire County Council, the Vale of White Horse District Council and Radley Parish Council.

Key features

Radley Church, dedicated to the apostle St James the Great, is located to the north-west of the village at the junction of Church Road and Kennington Road. It stands within the Green Belt on slightly higher ground than the main part of the village and overlying a small area of gravel that is part of the Wolvercote or Third Terrace, a river deposit during the Ice Age.[1] Nearby is the Vicarage, the Church Room and Radley Church of England Primary School, which has around 130 pupils aged 3 to 11. Radley has a flourishing community shop, a well-used village hall and a popular pub, but sadly no longer a post office. The village is well served with transport links, with a station on the main railway line between Oxford and Didcot, and a regular bus service between Oxford and Abingdon.

Radley Primary School   **Radley Village Shop**   **Bowyer Arms**

The River Thames forms the boundary of Radley to the east and south (see Map 1). To the south-west, the road around the Peachcroft housing estate in Abingdon marks the boundary of the civil parish. Radley College, an independent boys' boarding school with some 700 pupils, occupies an 800-acre campus to the north-west of the Church. Beyond the College, the busy A34 dual carriageway cuts through the corner of the parish. The railway line divides Lower Radley from the main village, much of which was built in the 1930s, 1950s and 1960s, with smaller developments in the 1980s and 1990s. Some houses dating from the sixteenth and seventeenth centuries (some with thatched roofs) can still be seen in Lower Radley, which until the 1930s was the main part of the village. The village also has four mobile home parks, three at the northern end near Kennington and one just over the railway bridge in Lower Radley. The station, the shop and the Bowyer Arms are all in the central area of the village.

---

[1] Most of the central area of Radley overlies the Second or Summertown–Radley Terrace, while Lower Radley and Thrupp are on the First or Floodplain Terrace.

At the southern end, Thrupp Lane leads to some light industrial units and Radley's lakes and gravel workings.

Area of Radley

Radley extends in all directions for some way from the centre of the village. The censuses between 1901 and 1931 record the area of the civil parish as 3,705 acres but, in 1951, as only 2,876 acres, Kennington having become a separate civil entity in 1936. The figure of 2,644 acres in the 2011 Census reflects the change to the boundary in 1986 as the boundary of Abingdon was extended to accommodate new housing estates.

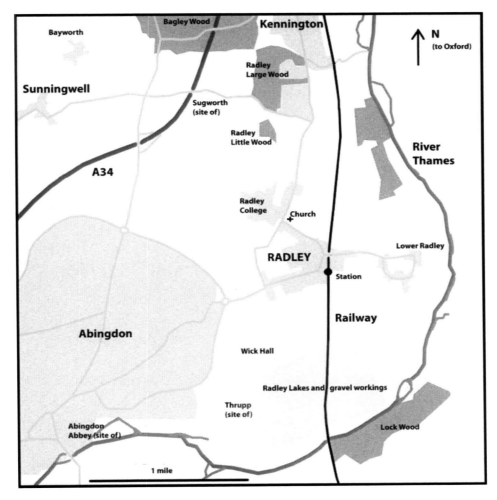

Map 1: Location of Radley

Away from the centre of the village

The built-up area of the village is surrounded by Green Belt land, some of which at the time of writing is under threat from proposed housing developments. Popular walks include: round the Lower Radley loop to the River Thames; through the grounds of Radley College to Radley Little Wood or across to Lodge Hill; the circular walk around Thrupp Lake;[2] south of

---

[2] A former gravel pit, it was saved by the local community in 2008 from becoming a disposal site for fly ash from Didcot Power Station. It is now managed as a nature reserve by the Earth Trust.

Thrupp Lake along the route of the former railway branch line to Abingdon; and along the towpath from the Radley College boathouse to Abingdon in one direction and Oxford in the other.

The population of Radley over the years

Research suggests that there were 200-275 people in Radley in the mid seventeenth century, living in 40-55 houses. A survey in 1811 found 337 people in 42 houses with 66 households. At the 1831 Census there were 515 people living in 87 houses; of the 93 families, 76 were recorded as being chiefly employed in agriculture. This gradual but slow increase in the number of inhabitants continued for the rest of the nineteenth century, reaching 592 in the 1901 Census. The population rose more quickly during the twentieth century from 927 in the 1911 Census to 1,675 in the 1961 Census and 2,835 in the 2011 Census. In 2011, there were 1,002 households and 641 people recorded as 'living in a communal establishment' (Radley College); 70% of residents gave their religion as Christian. The village currently has some 650 homes in the main settlement and 250-300 mobile homes in the three parks to the south of Kennington.

The ecclesiastical parish of Radley today

The ecclesiastical parish, the basic territorial unit in the Church of England, is the area served by the parish church, while the civil parish is the smallest unit of local government. In many places these areas are identical. For Radley, they are very similar but with some small differences. These arise primarily because the boundary of the civil parish has been adjusted over the years to reflect the pattern of new development while the ecclesiastical boundary (Map 2) has remained relatively unchanged.

Ecclesiastical parishes originated in medieval times when they indicated the area of land whose occupiers had to pay a tithe (a proportion of their annual produce or income) to the church. In the seventeenth century, these units began to be distinguished from civil parishes, which were the areas that could levy a poor rate. This divergence was formalised by several local government acts at the end of the nineteenth century, by which time less than a third of ecclesiastical parishes had a boundary coinciding with that of the corresponding civil parish.

Starting in the north-east at Sandford Lock, the ecclesiastical boundary of Radley follows the course of the River Thames. After a while it shifts to the far side of the river for a short way, following the district boundary between the Vale of the White Horse and South Oxfordshire and the line of the boundary between Berkshire and Oxfordshire before 1974. This piece of land (A in Map 2) was described as a meadow, 'Heardeight', in the land Terrier of Radley (a register of land holdings) in 1633 and 'Herd Eyott' in the 1849 tithe map.

The boundary then follows the towpath until it reaches the outskirts of Abingdon, with the exception of two small areas of land adjacent to the river (B and C in Map 2). John Rocque's 1762 map of Berkshire shows these two areas marked as 'To Abingdon', while the 25 inch Ordnance Survey map of 1875 shows them as two detached parts of the parish of St Helen's Church in Abingdon. These two areas were transferred to the civil parish of Radley on 24

March 1885 under the Local Government Board Order 18.177. These alterations to the civil parish boundary have not been adopted by the ecclesiastical authorities and so these small, uninhabited 'chunks' of land are still excluded from the ecclesiastical parish.

On leaving the Thames, the boundary extends around Longmead Lake (D in Map 2), a restored section of one of Radley's gravel pits, before running for a short distance along the disused railway line. As it heads north, the boundary generally follows the ancient field boundaries shown on the 1633 Terrier (see *Early Modern Radley: People, Land and Buildings 1547–1768* for details of the field structure at that time). As it does, it incorporates small parts of the built-up area of north-east Abingdon (E and F on Map 2). It also excludes an inverted L-shape of land (G on Map 2). This was formerly part of the parish of St Helen Without and is now part of the parish of North Abingdon, but is within the civil parish of Radley following the Berks Review Order 1934 – another change not adopted by the ecclesiastical authorities.

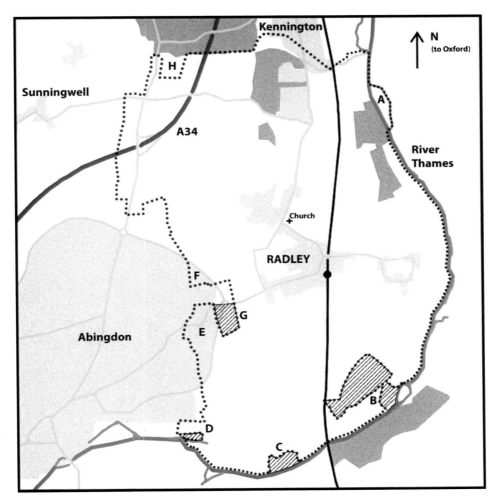

Map 2: Ecclesiastical boundary of Radley, 2015
See the text for details of the areas marked A to H

In the north, the boundaries of the ecclesiastical and civil parishes diverge in a number of places. The indented piece of land in the north-west corner (H on Map 2) is part of a former extra-parochial place,[3] Chandlings Farm, though it is within the civil parish of Radley. The boundaries run together along the southern edge of Bagley Wood, another former extra-parochial place. The ecclesiastical boundary then shifts slightly north through the outskirts of Kennington on its way back to the river at Sandford Lock,[4] while the boundary of the civil parish follows the northern edge of Radley Large Wood and then a little to the south of Sandford Lane.

The Stonhouses, Bowyers and Radley College

The names of Stonhouse, Bowyer and Radley College crop up throughout this book, so below is a brief synopsis of why. A simplified family tree of the Stonhouse and Bowyer families is given in Appendix 2.

Radley College is situated on land that in the medieval period was part of the Manor of Radley, which was owned by Abingdon Abbey. Following the dissolution of the Abbey by Henry VIII in 1538, the Manor of Radley was first granted to Thomas Seymour, Lord High Admiral of England, and then to Princess (later Queen) Elizabeth who sold the lordship of the Manor of Radley in 1560 to George Stonhouse, a Clerk of the Green Cloth (responsible for arranging royal journeys). He was succeeded in 1573 by his son William, who was created Baronet of Radley in 1628. The Stonhouse monument in Radley Church (see Chapter 3) commemorates both Sir William and his eldest son, John, the second baronet who died just a few months after his father in 1632.

The third baronet, John's younger brother George, was the MP for Abingdon from 1640 until January 1644 when he was barred from Parliament for being a Royalist supporter. He was forced to pay a considerable fine to retain his estates, but was re-elected as MP in 1660, holding the seat until his death in 1675. In 1670 he attempted to disinherit his eldest son, also George, by obtaining a new patent of baronetcy and becoming the first baronet of the 1670 creation. His second son, John, succeeded to the estate as second baronet of the new creation and as MP for Abingdon, while elder brother George made a successful claim to become the fourth baronet of the original creation. John's son, another John, became the third baronet of the 1670 creation in 1700. He was elected as MP for Berkshire in 1701 and served as Comptroller of the Royal Household for 1713-14, being appointed a Privy Counsellor in 1713. In the 1720s, Sir John built a grand Georgian style mansion known as Radley Hall to replace the existing manor house. In the early 1770s, 'Capability' Brown was paid for work in landscaping the grounds of Radley Hall.[5]

---

[3] An extra-parochial area or place is a geographically defined area outside the jurisdiction of any parish. Such areas had no church or clergy, and were exempt from paying poor rates and often tithes.

[4] The ecclesiastical parish of Kennington was created in 1866 (the village's church having previously been a chapel of Sunningwell Church), some 70 years before the civil parish was formed.

[5] It is not known exactly what this work involved, but the grounds of Radley College are an attributed and definite Capability Brown site. Elements of his design are still visible.

Sir John Stonhouse died in October 1733 a few months after his fourth daughter, Anne, married Sir William Bowyer Bt of Denham Court, Buckinghamshire, in Radley Church. He was succeeded by his eldest son, John, in whom the Stonhouse baronetcies were united in 1740 following the death of his unmarried cousin, another John, the sixth baronet of the original creation. Sir John was succeeded in turn by his two unmarried brothers, Sir William and the Revd Sir James Stonhouse (see Chapter 5). When Sir James died in 1792, the Radley estate went first to their niece, Penelope, Lady Rivers (daughter of Anne's eldest sister Penelope) and then in January 1795 to her cousin, Anne's third son, Sir George Bowyer, an officer in the British Navy. On the 'Glorious First of June' in 1794, Rear-Admiral George Bowyer lost a leg at the Third Battle of Ushant off Brest (the first naval action between Great Britain and France during the French Revolutionary Wars) in which he commanded HMS Barfleur. In recognition of his bravery he was made a vice-admiral, given a pension and created 1st Baronet Bowyer of Radley. Sir George was appointed admiral in 1799 and died in 1800. He was succeeded by his son George, 2nd Baronet of Radley, who got into severe financial difficulties primarily due to futile efforts to find coal on his land at Bayworth. The contents of Radley Hall were sold in 1815 and Sir George took his family to live in Italy. He died abroad in 1860 and is buried in the family vault in Radley churchyard (see Chapter 4). The various memorials to the Bowyer family inside the Church are described in Chapter 3.

In 1819, Radley Hall and 112 acres of parkland were leased to Benjamin Kent who ran a nonconformist school there until 1844. In 1847, a 21-year lease (later renewed to run to 1910) was given to Revd William Sewell and Robert Singleton for the site of their new public school, St Peter's College. Singleton became the first Warden (headmaster) of the school, now known as Radley College.

In 1860, a third Sir George Bowyer inherited the Radley Hall estate. A lawyer and Liberal politician, he was MP for Dundalk and then for Wexford County. After becoming a Roman Catholic in 1850, he devoted the rest of his life to the Catholic Church and was a generous philanthropist. He was a benefactor of the Church of Our Lady and St Edmund in Abingdon and founder of the Church of St John of Jerusalem in Great Ormond Street, London. He was a generous patron of Radley Church (see Chapter 3) and, in 1872, granted the vicar and churchwardens of Radley a 99-year lease on the land on which the village school stood. He died unmarried in 1883 and is buried in the family vault.

In July 1889, the family's debts forced Sir George's childless brother, Sir William Bowyer, then living in Brighton, to put Radley Hall and 1,277 acres of the Radley Hall estate (representing most, but not all, the land owned by the family) up for sale by auction. The main purchaser was Mrs Josephine Dockar-Drysdale of Wick Hall who, by prior arrangement, immediately sold the freehold of Radley Hall and 136 acres of Radley Park to the trustees of Radley College. Sir William died in 1893 and was succeeded by his nephew, Sir George Henry, who had no children and the Radley baronetcy became extinct on his death in 1950. The simplified family tree of the Stonhouses and Bowyers in Appendix 2 shows the relationships between the various lords of the Manor of Radley.

In 1897, Sir William's sister, Miss Mary Bowyer, who was then living in Florence, gave the vicar and churchwardens the freehold of all the school land and the buildings covered by the 1872 lease, plus land on the approach to the church to enlarge the churchyard (see Chapter 4). Mrs Dockar-Drysdale died in 1921 and, when a large part of the Wick Hall estate came on the market in 1930, Radley College purchased 302 acres. Further land acquisitions over the years have made it a major landowner in Radley.

The names of the Stonhouse and Bowyer families live on in Radley, not only in and around Radley Church, but in two road names (Stonhouse Crescent and Bowyer Close) and the village pub, the Bowyer Arms.

A short ecclesiastical history of the parish of Radley

When the current church was built around 1300, Radley was in the Diocese of Salisbury ('Sarum'), which was created in 1219, and covered Dorset, Wiltshire and Berkshire. Radley Church did not have independent status but was a 'chapel' of St Helen's Church in Abingdon, itself under the jurisdiction of Abingdon Abbey. Henry VIII's reforms in 1540 to 1542, following the dissolution of the monasteries, created a new Diocese of Oxford but Radley remained in the Diocese of Salisbury. The next major reform between 1835 and 1849 was much more significant for Radley, as Berkshire and some parts of Wiltshire were transferred to the Diocese of Oxford along with Buckinghamshire from the Diocese of Lincoln.

Today the Diocese of Oxford contains 815 churches spread around Berkshire, Buckinghamshire and Oxfordshire, more than any other diocese in the Church of England. Radley Church is part of the Abingdon deanery.[6] Abingdon and the other three 'old Berkshire' deaneries of Wallingford, Wantage and the Vale of White Horse were part of the Archdeaconry of Berkshire under the Bishop of Reading until 1 March 2014 when they moved to the new Archdeaconry of Dorchester under the Bishop of Dorchester. This change aligned the diocese's four archdeaconries (Oxford, Buckingham, Dorchester and Reading) to better reflect civil boundaries.

As explained in Chapter 5, Radley Church was apparently independent from St Helen's by the seventeenth century with the Stonhouses appointing the vicar, though formal separation was not until the mid nineteenth century. Chapter 5 also details the dispute with the Bishop of Oxford in the 1860s over the legal right to appoint the vicar; Sir George Bowyer and Radley College, to whom he had sold the right to appoint the next three vicars, took the view that the Bishop had no say in the matter. In 1892, Radley College acquired the permanent right to appoint the vicar (the 'advowson') from Miss Mary Bowyer in exchange for Radley Little Wood. The College purchased the wood back again through its Land Fund the following year.

---

[6] A deanery is a group of neighbouring parishes forming an administrative area, overseen by the Area or Rural Dean (an ordained minister), who is normally the incumbent of a parish within the deanery, and a lay chair (not ordained).

The late 1980s saw a significant change for the church in Radley when the parishes of St James the Great, Radley and St Leonard's, Sunningwell were united to create the 'Benefice of Radley and Sunningwell'.[7] This merger came at a time of many amalgamations of rural parishes as the Church of England, against a backdrop of a general decline in church attendance, sought to deal with the challenges posed by falling numbers of clergy and stretched resources. The Pastoral Scheme made by the Church Commissioners on 9 October 1990 stated that Radley and Sunningwell would continue to be distinct parishes but that the incumbent (the ordained minister) of the new benefice would live in Radley Vicarage. It also stipulated that the 'right of presentation to the new benefice shall be exercised alternately by Radley College, … which shall have the first turn, and the Oxford Diocesan Board of Patronage'.

Since then the process of appointing the incumbent has followed the Church of England's guidance on parochial appointments, which gives much more say to church members. The Parochial Church Council (PCC) (or a small subgroup of the PCC) prepares a profile of the parish, draws up the job specification and appoints two parish representatives. The interview panel is made up of two representatives from each parish to be served by the new vicar together with representatives of the bishop and the patron. Significantly, the appointment made by the interview panel requires the consent of the parish representatives, and neither the bishop nor the patron can 'over-rule the veto of one of the PCC representatives'.

More recently, a Pastoral Scheme dated 26 February 2015 united the benefice of Radley and Sunningwell with the benefice of St Swithun's, Kennington, to form the 'Benefice of Radley, Sunningwell and Kennington'. Radley Vicarage was designated as the residence of the incumbent of the new benefice. The Pastoral Scheme states that the 'right of presentation to the new benefice shall, on each occasion, be exercised jointly by the Bishop of Oxford in a corporate capacity, the Diocesan Board of Patronage, and Radley College'.

Sources

Books by Radley History Club

Early Modern Radley: People, Land and Buildings 1547-1768, Richard Dudding, 2014

Radley Farms and Families, 1600-2011, Christine Wootton, 2011

The Changing Boundaries of Radley and Sunningwell Parishes, Stanley Baker and Peter McWhirter, 2014

The History of Radley, Patrick Drysdale, Rita Ford, Patricia Groser, Marian Orchard, Ann Parkes and Kay Williams, 2002

The History of Radley CE Primary School, Christine Wootton, 2008

Other books

Radley. Ancient Barrows to Modern Parish, Patrick Drysdale, 1985

The History of Radley College 1847-1947, A.K. Boyd, 1948

---

[7] A benefice is a parish or group of parishes, normally under the care of a single stipendiary (paid) minister.

Documents

Appointment of Clergy Office Holders: A Guide to Good Practice, Church of England Remuneration and Conditions of Service Committee, 2015

Dioceses and Episcopal Sees in England: A Background Report for the Dioceses Commission, Colin Podmore, Chapter 2, 2008

Examination of Vale of White Horse Local Plan 2013: Part 1 Strategic Sites and Policies. Submission by Radley Parish Council: August 2015

Inspection report of Radley Church of England Primary School, March 2015, Ofsted

Pastoral Scheme uniting the benefices of Radley and Sunningwell in the Diocese of Oxford, Church Commissioners, 9 October 1990 (Order in Council dated 31 October 1990)

Pastoral Scheme uniting the benefice of Radley and Sunningwell and the benefice of Saint Swithun, Kennington in the Diocese of Oxford, Church Commissioners, 26 January 2015

Websites

A Church Near You, Parish Finder, www.achurchnearyou.com/parishfinder.php

A Vision of Britain Through Time, www.visionofbritain.org.uk

Abingdon-on-Thames, www.abingdon.gov.uk

Capability Brown, www.capabilitybrown.org

Cracroft's Peerage, www.cracroftspeerage.co.uk

Diocese of Oxford, www.oxford.anglican.org

Diocese of Salisbury, www.salisbury.anglican.org

National Heritage List for England, https://historicengland.org.uk/listing/the-list/

History of Parliament, www.historyofparliamentonline.org

Nomis – official labour market statistics, www.nomisweb.co.uk/census/2011/ks101ew

Radley College, www.radley.org.uk

Radley History Club, www.radleyhistoryclub.org.uk

Radley Village, www.radleyvillage.org.uk

St Edmund's Church, Abingdon, www.stedmundabingdon.org.uk

St Swithun's Church, Kennington, www.stswithunskennington.org/history.htm

The Church of St John of Jerusalem, www.smom-za.org/gbsmomch.htm

The English Civil and Ecclesiastical Parish – A Brief History, www.metadyne.co.uk/Parish.html

The Peerage, www.thepeerage.com

The Telegraph, www.telegraph.co.uk/news/earth/greenpolitics/planning/9708387/Interactive-map-Englands-green-belt.html

Wikipedia, https://en.wikipedia.org

Photographs courtesy of John Huddleston

Chapter 2: Origins and Buildings

by Richard Dudding

Early origins

The current Church of Saint James the Great, Radley, was consecrated around 1300 AD and the Vicarage dates back to a similar period. They are by a considerable margin the oldest buildings still standing in the village. The Church's origins go back even further, as there was an earlier building, about which we know practically nothing, dating back to Norman or even Saxon times. It was reputedly destroyed by fire.

What do we know about these early origins and how do they relate to Radley as a place? Radley was at that time an agrarian community, with almost all the population consisting of serfs and villeins who worked the land in a feudal relationship to the lord of the Manor. The Manor of Radley was held by Abingdon Abbey, some three miles to the south-west. The Abbey had been reputedly founded in about 700 AD and certainly before the Norman Conquest. Until its dissolution in 1538 it was the dominant force in North Berkshire, not just as a religious house but as a holder of land and power. The Abbey held 'domain' land in Radley for its own use, and this included an enclosed park which provided game and timber. The majority of land in Radley, however, was worked by the local people for their own use in return for labour services and other feudal dues owed to the Abbey.

Radley Church did not have independent status but was a 'chapel' of St Helen's Church in Abingdon. The vicar of St Helen's was appointed by the Abbey and he was in turn required to provide a chaplain for Radley. A detailed deed of 1271 sets out these arrangements, which would have applied when the current church was built.[1]

As shown in Figure 2.1, Radley at this time did not have a single nucleus but consisted of four settlements with their own distinct boundaries and characteristics. The Domesday Book of 1087 is not helpful in telling us about these settlements as all except Sugworth, which gets its own mention, were subsumed in Barton – the Abbey's 'home' group of manors.[2] But we know more from taxation records made soon after. In a tax assessment of *c.*1200, Radley is shown as a settlement of 15 ploughs and is distinguished from Thrupp and Sugworth, which were assessed at three and four ploughs respectively.[3] This makes Radley one of the larger settlements in North Berkshire and certainly large enough to justify the building of a church.

---

[1] Radley formally remained a chaplaincy of St Helen's until the nineteenth century, but in practice was largely independent by the seventeenth century (see Chapter 5).

[2] Barton included not only Radley and nearby villages such as Sunningwell and Hinksey, but also Abingdon itself. The grouping reflects the way they were managed as an entity by the Abbey, which held the relevant manors directly. The reason why Sugworth gets its own mention in the Domesday Book is probably because the Abbey had devolved Sugworth Manor (see Figure 2.1).

[3] A plough was the area of land which could be worked by a team of eight oxen, typically about 100 acres.

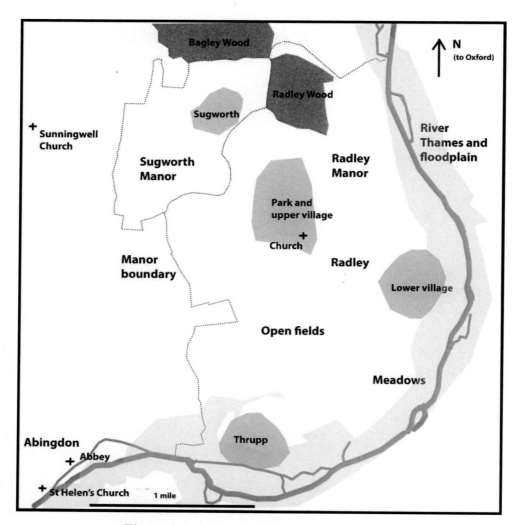

Figure 2.1: Settlements in medieval Radley

What is now the parish of Radley consisted of two manors: Radley and the smaller one of Sugworth to the north-west. The population was spread between the four settlements indicated in medium shading: the upper village near the Church, the lower village (now Lower Radley) and the hamlets of Sugworth and Thrupp. The light shading shows the extent of the floodplain.

Sugworth Manor at the time of the Domesday Book was held separately by a military tenant of the Abbey, called Warin. Within the manor, the settlement of Sugworth was near what later became Sugworth Farm. It appears to have remained very small and became totally deserted towards the end of the Middle Ages. Thrupp, near the Thames floodplain to the south, had a more continuing presence in its own right and, by the end of the thirteenth century, paid almost as much tax as the main part of Radley. But soon after it declined sharply in size and was largely deserted by the seventeenth century.

We would not have expected a church to be built at Sugworth or Thrupp, but it is puzzling why Radley Church was built where it is rather than nearer the River Thames in the lower village – Lower Radley as it is now called. This is where most of Radley's old houses are and, until the twentieth century, was the largest part of the village.

One possible explanation is that Lower Radley was prone to flooding and was not considered a robust location for a substantial structure such as a church. This has some plausibility except that it does not explain why Radley Church was built nearly a mile from Lower Radley. Solid ground above the floodplain could have been found much closer.

Another possible explanation is that the site of the Church was chosen to be near the manor house on the hill above it. The site, however, would have been chosen when the Abbey held the lordship of the Manor and there is no evidence that they had any building of status where the Stonhouses later built their residence.

A more plausible explanation for the Church's location is that the surrounding area was relatively well populated when it was first sited there and that this population later shrank and/or migrated to Lower Radley. The current Church was not the first one in Radley. It replaced one that was reputedly destroyed by fire. There is evidence of Norman elements in the current structure and it seems fairly likely that the site of the Church was chosen in Norman or even Saxon times, when settlement patterns might have been rather different.

Lower Radley has the look of a planned settlement, with farmsteads in a regular pattern round a circular road, rather than one which grew more randomly, and it must be possible that the population migrated there at some point rather than grew organically. It is tempting to think that this might have been the result of the Black Death of 1348 to 1349, which killed about a third of the population of England and led directly or indirectly to many settlements shrinking or becoming deserted. There is, however, no evidence of the Black Death being particularly severe in Radley or the wider Abingdon area.[4] It looks therefore that we need to go back even further in time for why the settlement at Lower Radley developed.

One possible factor is the creation by the Abbey of Radley Park. This was an area of its domain land fenced off for the management of timber and game, under the custody of a park keeper. We do not know the precise location or size of this park, but it was almost certainly on the higher ground above the Church where the manor house was later sited. We do know that Radley Park was already in existence in 1260, when John le Parker was appointed as park keeper,[5] and a record of 1387 shows that the area included six 'tofts' and one 'messuage' (a home and outbuildings), presumably the park keeper's. Tofts are the sites of former houses, so here is evidence of there having been a settlement which then became deserted. The creation of Radley Park might therefore have been a contributory factor, even if not the sole explanation, for the area of Radley near the Church becoming depopulated.

---

[4] Taxation records for Radley (excluding Thrupp) suggest that the number of households did not fall significantly around the time of the Black Death. The records of Abingdon Abbey are remarkably free of references to the disease, unlike many other chronicles of the period. However, this does not mean that there was no material impact and it is particularly striking that the Abingdon churches of St Helen's and St Nicolas' had six new rectors and vicars in 1349 compared with only one in the period between 1337 and 1346. The clergy suffered disproportionately during the Black Death.

[5] This is a good example of a surname being adopted to reflect a trade.

The building of the current Church

Radley Church has evolved over the centuries, with the earliest parts of the current structure dating to about 1300 and the porch having been added as recently as 1877.[6] Figure 2.2 shows Radley Church as it is today and Figure 2.3 shows a plan of the Church.

Figure 2.2: Radley Church pictured from the south-east and the west

---

[6] There is evidence from pre 1877 maps of Radley that there was an earlier porch in the same position, in which case the current porch must be a replacement.

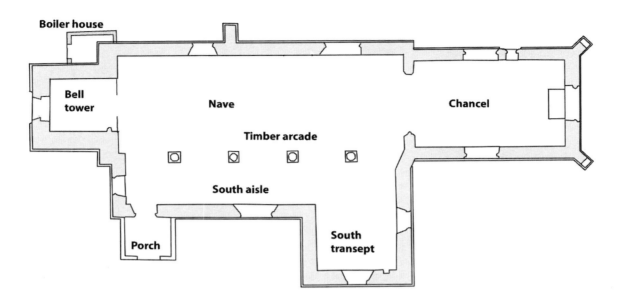

Figure 2.3: Plan of the Church

There is some uncertainty about the precise date of original construction. Prior to the major restoration project in 1902, a survey was carried out in 1899 by the diocesan architect, C. Oldrid Scott. He considered that the oldest part of the building was the south transept, which he described as 'untouched work of the beginning of the fourteenth century'. Historic England also gives the Church a fourteenth century date in its National Heritage List for England. However, a date between 1292 and 1297 is now normally given. The evidence for this earlier dating is the consecration cross, now set in the sill of the west window of the aisle,[7] which bears the inscription 'NSM'. It seems likely that this indicates the name of the bishop who performed the consecration ceremony – N Sarum. Radley was in the Diocese of Salisbury, often referred to as Sarum, and the only 'N' who was bishop around this time was Nicolas Longspée, who held the see from 1292 to 1297. The earlier Church was still in existence in 1271 (we know this from the deed of that year referred to above), so it must have burnt down soon after.

It is likely that some of the stone from the earlier building was incorporated in the new structure: on the north-east side of the current building there is a Norman corbel, and the font is also late Norman (see Chapter 3). Equally there have been significant additions since the new Church was consecrated. The tower, nave and south aisle seem likely to have been constructed in the fifteenth century. Some evidence about the evolution is provided by the windows shown in Figure 2.4. Those in the south transept are Early English in style, consistent with Scott's comments about the transept's fourteenth century construction. Those in the nave and south aisle are Perpendicular in style, suggesting construction of this part of the Church in the fifteenth century. Confusingly the windows in the chancel are also

---

[7] This would not have been part of the original construction, so the stone must have moved there at some stage.

Perpendicular. The chancel of a church would normally be built before the transept, so it seems likely that the chancel was largely rebuilt at much the same time as the nave was built.

Figure 2.4: Early English window in south face of south transept (left) and Perpendicular window in south aisle (right)

The Early English window dates to the 1902 restoration but probably follows the style of the original.

The evidence from the stonework is that the tower was constructed last of all. The stone of most of the building is uncoursed rubble and crude. The tower stonework is 'ashlar', meaning it is much more refined with the stones fine cut and dressed. They were probably quarried in Sunningwell, which was the source of a good quality hard stone. The tower appears to have been added rather than constructed as part of an integrated whole, as shown in Figure 2.5.

Figure 2.5: Stonework, north side of church

On the left is the crude uncoursed rubble of the aisle. On the right is the finely cut ashlar of the tower. In between is a buttress, also of ashlar. The tower and buttress appear to have been grafted on to the west end of the Church.

Probably the Church's most notable feature is the fine arcade of oak pillars between the nave and south aisle which support the roof structure (Figure 2.6). The use of wood rather than stone is unusual, even in an area such as Radley where good quality oak was plentiful. There is a story that the abbot of Abingdon, faced with the need to rebuild the church, had a vision in which he was instructed to 'seek pillars in the forest', but documentary evidence is absent.

There are not only timber pillars supporting the south side of the roof but also timber arches spanning the nave (Figure 2.6). As described later in the chapter, the latter are not original but were erected in 1902. But it appears from mortice holes in the timber pillars that there were similar timber arches as part of the original nave structure. These must have been removed during an earlier re-roofing, most likely in 1703. Figure 2.7 shows how the nave looked after this re-roofing and before the restoration of 1902.

Figure 2.6: Nave today looking east towards the chancel, with two of the pillars visible on the right.

Figure 2.7: Nave looking east before the 1902 restoration (© Oxfordshire History Centre)

Scott, in his 1899 report prior to the 1902 restoration, was very critical of the Church as it appeared then. He remarked that the roof above the nave and south aisle was 'more recent and without architectural character' and that the chancel had been renovated to some extent, with recent buttresses, parapets and pinnacles. He also believed that considerable restoration work had been carried out some 60 years previously[8] and that this had been unsympathetic.

On the south and west sides of the tower are sun dials, which would have enabled passing villagers to tell the time of day. Much less visible but more intriguing there are also two 'mass dials' scratched into the stonework, one by the south transept window (see Figure 2.8) and one by the west door in the tower.[9] The precise origin of these is uncertain, but similar dials are found in a number of medieval churches. It is believed that their purpose was to act as service markers to help the priest measure the intervals between the services that made up the canonical hours. They do not seem very practical and it may be that the dials also had some mystical significance. A wooden stick, called a gnomon, would have been inserted in the centre, casting a shadow. The holes round the circumference and the lines pointing to them indicated the times of the various services.

Figure 2.8: Mass dial by the south transept window

Stonework decorating the church exterior includes a floral cornice along the top of the chancel wall (probably dating to around 1300), and two gargoyles and two grotesques on the corners of the tower (probably fifteenth century) (Figure 2.9).

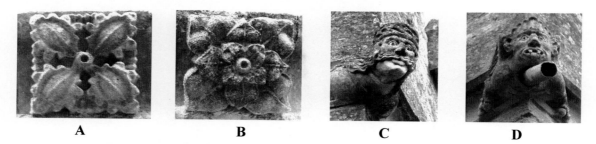

| A | B | C | D |

Figure 2.9: Floral decorations on the chancel wall (A, B) and grotesque (C) and gargoyle (D) on the tower

---

[8] The Berkshire volume of the Pevsner Architecture Guides to the buildings of England refers to 'major alterations' having been carried out *c.*1839 to 1847, including the introduction of 'excellent woodwork and stained glass'. If Scott was referring to this work, there seems to be a difference of view about its appropriateness.

[9] It is surprising to find a mass dial on the west side of the Church, because the dial would need to face south to function properly, and it is probable it was moved during restoration work.

The Church is asymmetric: there is no north aisle and no north transept matching those on the south. The roof structure is supported on the north side not by wooden pillars but by the external wall. This asymmetry is curious and the prevailing view has been that the Church was originally built with a north aisle and transept but that these were demolished following damage in a Civil War skirmish of 1643. The evidence for this is considered in the next section.

Civil War, aisle and transept

During the Civil War, Radley was close to the heart of the fighting. In 1643 the Royalists had their headquarters at Oxford, held Abingdon, and also had a major encampment on Culham Hill over the river from Radley. Soldiers were billeted not just there but in the nearby villages, quite often using the churches, and it seems very likely that Radley Church was host to Royalist soldiers at this time. In May 1644, Abingdon was taken by the Parliamentarians, without a fight and as the result of poor communication on the Royalist side. The Royalists then made three unsuccessful attempts to retake Abingdon – the last in 1646 involving an advance through Radley. It is known that two officers and several troopers were buried in Radley churchyard in July 1643 and it is believed that one or both of the officers were buried in the panelled chest tomb near the Church porch known today at the Cavalier's tomb (see Chapter 4).

A tradition has grown up that these deaths were the result of a skirmish in the churchyard, and furthermore that the Church suffered major damage. When C. Oldrid Scott wrote his report in 1899 on the state of the Church he said:

> The Nave is reported to have had a North Aisle as well as a South till the time of the Civil Wars, when the North side was destroyed. The roof must have disappeared at the same time, the present covering of the Nave and South Aisle being more recent.

A short leaflet about the Church written at the same time as part of fundraising for the impending restoration said that the roof and aisle were destroyed between 1644 and 1650 and rebuilt between c. 1670 and 1690.

The Victoria County History (VCH) of Berkshire, written in 1924, says that the 'north aisle and transept of the nave' were destroyed in the Civil War and that the foundations of both were 'recently discovered'. Although the VCH is generally meticulous in referencing its statements, no source is given for this, indicating that it might be based on an oral report. The VCH also refers to an inscription on the east side of the tower above the roof that 'H Perrin flattened this roof 1703'.

Clarke and Colvin in their 1952 book on the restoration of Berkshire churches say that the Church was 'badly decayed' in 1643 and that the north wall was not rebuilt until 1702, seemingly linking this point to the Perrin inscription about the roof.

Sydney Allso, then Vicar of Radley, wrote in 1971 that the north aisle and transept were destroyed by Parliamentary troops in 1643. He also says that foundations of the north aisle and transept were found during the 1902 restoration. However, he goes on to challenge the view (presumably that of Clarke and Colvin) that the Church remained a roofless ruin until 1703. He puts this down to a misinterpretation of the 1703 inscription that 'H. Perrin flattened this roof'. He argues that Lenthall's pulpit canopy (see Chapter 3) was erected in 1653 and that this could not possibly have survived in a roofless church.

The latest (2010) edition of the Berkshire volume of Pevsner Architectural Guides states that there had been Civil War damage in 1643, that the north wall was not rebuilt until 1702, and that the roof was rebuilt in the following year. No source is cited, but this is essentially the same account as given in 1952 by Clarke and Colvin and the author of the relevant Pevsner passage has confirmed in correspondence that it was taken directly from it.

Unfortunately, none of these accounts are backed by direct evidence or even quote sources. The sections below look forensically at such limited evidence as is available – architectural, archaeological and historical – to consider what is most likely to have happened.

Architectural evidence

Architecturally it would normally be expected that a church built at the time of St James the Great, Radley, would be symmetrical. An aisle on one side of the nave would typically be matched by one on the other, and there would typically be a transept on each side so as to give the shape of a cross. Observation of the current structure of Radley Church arguably supports the view that there was once a north aisle. It seems odd to have an arcade of pillars on one side of the aisle, a striking feature, without that being matched on the other. It is also notable that the apex of the roof is set slightly to one side of the nave (see Figures 2.6 and 2.7), which would be consistent with the wall on the north side of the aisle not being an original structure.

If there had once been a north aisle and this had been destroyed, it would in principle have been feasible to build a new stone wall keeping the timber pillars in place to support the roof while this was being done. There is some suggestion in the wall's stonework that it has indeed been built later than the rest of the nave. The two windows in this new wall would need to have been salvaged from the original outer wall unless they were replacements in the same style.

None of this architectural evidence is however decisive. The stonework of Radley Church has been chopped and changed so much over the centuries that a definitive interpretation of its evolution is not possible. Not all churches moreover were built symmetrically. Without travelling far, you can find asymmetrical churches at Steventon and South Leigh, both of similar date and it is generally accepted that they have always been asymmetric.

Archaeological evidence

Archaeologically there is some limited evidence to support the prior existence of a north aisle and transept. During the 1902 restoration the ground level outside the current north wall was lowered to reduce damp, and there were later reports that foundations of a north aisle were encountered during this work. If contemporary first-hand reports of this were available it might be conclusive, but nothing has so far come to light. There have also been accounts of musket balls and a cannon ball (Figure 2.10) having been found in the churchyard, of musket imprints being found in the Church tower, and a suggestion that stones from the Civil War damage to the Church might be present in the churchyard wall.

Figure 2.10: Cannon ball reputedly found in the churchyard
The ball has a diameter of about 10 cm (4 inches) and weighs about 4 kg (9 lbs). A ball of this size, known as a 'nine pounder', would have been fired by a demi-culverin, weighing about 1,500 kg (3,300 lbs). Such a weapon was not one to be used in a light skirmish.

But there is a lack of direct evidence to substantiate these accounts or to link them directly to major structural damage to the Church in the Civil War. For example, some of the stones in the churchyard wall may quite possibly be from the Church, but over the centuries, much of the Church's stonework has been replaced through various restorations, so their presence does not provide direct evidence in relation to an aisle and transept or to the Civil War period.

In 2014 Radley History Club commissioned a geophysical survey to test whether evidence could be found of the foundations of a north aisle and transept. Figure 2.11 shows the survey in progress. If foundations still existed they would have been expected to show up as areas of high resistance. Although the survey produced clear readings, it concluded that:

> Subject to the usual caveats of geophysics being far from infallible, we did not find any trace of linear areas of high resistance which one would expect for the demolition rubble and footings of a former aisle or transept in this area.

It might be argued that if workmen encountered foundations during the 1902 restoration they could have removed them and that is why the 2014 survey did not detect them. But church foundations are normally substantial and it seems unlikely that the removal would have been so complete as to leave no geophysical trace. It seems particularly unlikely that transept foundations were found and removed in 1902, as the lowering of the ground required for the restoration did not impinge on the area where a north transept would have been. There are moreover nineteenth century graves in this area, so it is difficult to see how restoration work in 1902 could have removed any transept foundations.

Figure 2.11: Geophysical survey being carried out by Roger and Sally Ainslie of Abingdon Archaeological Geophysics, 13 November 2014

The balance of archaeological evidence so far available therefore points against the Church ever having had a north aisle and transept, with the greater doubt attaching to the transept.

Historical evidence

The historical evidence is clear on one point: there is no foundation for the tradition that the aisle and transept were destroyed in 1643 in a skirmish which also led to the death of Royalists officers and soldiers. There were no Parliamentary troops in the vicinity until well into 1644. It seems much more likely that the Royalist troops buried in Radley in 1643 died from disease, which was rife at the time.[10]

If there was Civil War damage arising from fighting, it must have been in some separate incident between 1644 and 1646 when troops of both sides were in the area. Such an incident must have been on a significantly large enough scale to have involved cannon, which would have been needed to bring down church walls. On 28 May 1644, Parliamentary troops under the Earl of Essex moved north from Abingdon towards the east side of Oxford. They crossed the river at Sandford, which suggests their route took them through Radley, but there is no

---

[10] There were 43 burials in Radley in 1643, of which 40 were between May and September and 21 in July. This rate was quite exceptional. There were only 40 burials in the whole of the 1630s. It is difficult to be sure how many of the burials were of soldiers as ranks are given only for the officers. However, 11 of the burials in July 1643, including the two officers, were of people with unfamiliar surnames. That still leaves over 30 villagers being buried in 1643, a number well in excess of the norm and indicative of disease. There was also an exceptional level of deaths from disease in Abingdon at this time. A further possibility is that Radley Church was being used to store powder and an explosion occurred, as happened to the church at Sutton Courtenay in 1643, but an explosion of this scale would surely have been recorded at the time and there is no such record.

record of any fighting there. There were three attempts by the Royalists to retake Abingdon. The first was by a light skirmishing party at the end of May 1644, which might have passed through Radley but was unlikely to have involved significant fighting. The second in January 1645 did involve significant fighting but approached from Culham in the east, not through Radley. The third was another significant attack in March 1646 when Royalist troops advanced through Radley between Northcourt and Thrupp.[11] The troops, however, reached Abingdon undetected, so there cannot have been fighting in Radley en route. It is possible that there was fighting during the subsequent withdrawal, but the contemporary records do not mention this and certainly do not record damage to Radley's Church.

There is a further problem with theories based on action by Parliamentary troops. They were based in Abingdon to the south of the Church, yet it is the north aisle and transept that were reputedly destroyed. One account suggests that they were damaged in an attack from Sunningwell, which is to the north-west of the Church, and that Sunningwell supported the Parliamentary side. There is, however, no known evidence for Sunningwell's Parliamentary allegiance. On the contrary it was host to a Royalist military hospital. Nor is there any evidence of a Parliamentary attack from Sunningwell and it seems particularly unlikely that a force of sufficient strength to include cannon would have been based there.

An incident of sufficient scale to bring down a Church aisle and transept would surely have been recorded in journals of the time, but no record has been found either in Civil War accounts (for example, those of Anthony à Wood) or in documents relating to Radley. In respect of the latter the churchwardens' presentments have been examined, as these include a brief report each year on the condition of the Church. Unfortunately, there is a gap between 1641, when 'omnia' was 'bono', to 1666, when there is a return but no comment on the fabric. The first clear comment on the fabric is in 1672 when 'all things well and in good order.' No other contemporary documents reveal any clues.

Conclusions on the evidence

What conclusions can be drawn from this largely conflicting evidence?

It certainly must be possible, and arguably probable, that the Church never had a north aisle and transept. Parishioners might have wondered why their church was asymmetrical and perhaps a local tradition developed. It was known that Royalist troops billeted in the Church had been buried there in 1643 and their deaths by disease may have become spun into deaths

---

[11] David Eddershaw in his 1995 book on the Civil War in Oxfordshire asserts that Radley Church was damaged in this attack, but cites no evidence. Mieneke Cox in her 1993 history of Abingdon 1556-1702 says that the Church lost its aisle in the Civil War 'most likely in March 1646'. This is in a paragraph which also mentions two other instances of Civil War damage (Bayworth House and Sutton Courtenay Church). Cox is normally meticulous in citing sources and other evidence and in the latter two cases she does so. No source or evidence is however cited for damage to Radley Church – just as none is cited in other accounts. Her source for Bayworth House is Anthony à Wood of Oxford. Wood was a prolific contemporary diarist and chronicler with something to say on most subjects, especially if unfavourable to the Parliamentarians. He has nothing at all to say about Radley in the Civil War.

from a battle in the churchyard. By a further extension the supposed battle may have become spun into one in which the Church was severely damaged, and a dramatic story was thereby created to explain the mundane fact that the Church lacked a north aisle and transept.

The evidence for a north aisle and transept is indeed limited, but not so limited to be totally dismissed – especially in the case of the aisle. If they did originally exist when were they destroyed? This would almost certainly have been before 1703 when Perrin replaced the roof, but need not have been close to that date as their loss would not of itself have caused the main roof to collapse. The legend of a 1643 battle in the churchyard does not stand up and the evidence for damage later in the Civil War is also very thin. If they were destroyed it might have been a quite separate and earlier event (say in the sixteenth century) arising from poor construction. An earlier date would certainly help explain why there is no record of the damage having occurred.

Overall the present evidence seems evenly matched as to whether the Church ever had a north aisle and transept. It seems relatively unlikely that there was destruction in the Civil War, but the debate will continue and the tradition of a Civil War battle might be one to die hard. Any new evidence would be very welcome.

Anglo-Catholic plans in the 1890s

The Berkshire Record Office holds a series of plans for modifications to the Church drawn by F.C. Eden, architect of 3 Staple Inn, Holborn, London, dated June 1895. The drawings show:

- a new altar to Our Lady of Pity in the south transept;
- the organ being moved from the south transept to a new gallery above the entrance to the tower, with a new bell ringers' gallery on the same level behind;
- a new 'loft' above the south aisle to be accessed by stairs to the south of the chancel arch;
- a new screen separating the nave from the chancel and an elaborate 'rood beam' set in the chancel arch;
- a new sacristy (or vestry), built as an extension alongside the north side of the chancel and accessed by the chancel door.

None of these modifications happened and there is no documentary evidence to show why the plans were drawn up. There are however two clues. The first is that Frederick Charles Eden later became well-known as a church architect and his commissions were mainly for Anglo-Catholic churches. The second is that the drawings were made during a period (1893 to 1898) when Radley had two successive vicars, Charles Gore and James Nash,[12] who were founder members of the Community of the Resurrection which was then housed in the Vicarage. The Community had high Anglican beliefs, close in many ways to Roman Catholicism, and the best guess is that Gore and/or Nash commissioned these drawings to reflect their leanings but they were not pursued, due either to a lack of wider support or to funds being unavailable. As

---

[12] Details of the various incumbents mentioned in this chapter are given in the chronological listing of clergy in Chapter 5.

described below, the focus changed soon after from flamboyant modification to essential repair.

Restoration of 1902

In 1899 the new vicar, the Revd Charles Boxall Longland, noticed cracks in the Church walls. He consulted the Bishop of Oxford, who recommended he obtained advice from the diocesan architect, C. Oldrid Scott. Scott carried out a survey on 24 June 1899. His report recommended significant structural work as follows:

- underpinning the transept and aisle walls;
- resetting the chancel, nave and tower parapets;
- repairing and strengthening the nave wall;
- repairing the roof of the chancel, nave and tower;
- renewing the lead gutters and down spouts;
- lowering the ground around the church and properly draining it.

He also suggested some additional items, including a new and different kind of heating apparatus. Excluding these discretionary items he estimated the cost would be £880.

On 11 July a (thinly attended) public meeting was held in the parish room to consider the report. It was agreed to proceed with all the recommended works, but not to start until £500 had been raised. A restoration committee was elected to oversee the fundraising and the execution of the work, with the warden of Radley College (Revd Thomas Field) as chairman, the vicar as secretary and William Dockar-Drysdale of Wick Hall, whose mother Josephine was the principal landowner in the village (see Chapter 1), as treasurer. This committee met 11 times between July 1899 and November 1904, when its task was finally complete.

Scott drew up a detailed specification for the work and four tenders were received in June 1900. The lowest was £1,055 and the highest £1,114. The committee decided to accept the tender of Wyatt & Sons of Oxford, not just because this was the lowest but on account also of their proximity. Even this tender was above the £880 that Scott had estimated and there were to be further increases as the project progressed. The work on the chancel roof required a more comprehensive solution than allowed for and the bells were repaired. The final cost was £1,532 7s 10½d; as well as the works themselves, this sum included incidental costs on architect's fees, storage and fundraising.

Scott had recommended the re-introduction of oak arches across the nave roof. This was not structurally essential, but Scott believed it would 'greatly improve the appearance of the church'. The Committee decided not to proceed with this, but the present church does nevertheless have four timber arches spanning the roof. The answer lies in a plaque on the wall (see Chapter 3) saying that the arches were 'erected by Josephine Dockar-Drysdale' as a memorial to her father, William Dockar. A nice image is conjured of her lifting them into place herself, but the reference is clearly to the funding.

The most troublesome aspect of the works turned out to be the relatively mundane one of the heating system. In May 1902 the Committee considered two options: hot water and 'Grundy's system of hot air'. They decided firmly 'not to entertain hot air', but at their next meeting rescinded the decision on the advice of Scott. Grundy's hot air system was duly installed[13] but it turned out, to quote the committee, to be 'useless' as the stoke hole flooded. Attempts to put it right failed and a rather apologetic Scott advised that Wyatt & Sons should be asked to take over the work and that Grundy should not be paid. This advice was accepted and there is no report of any come-back from Grundy.

The restoration work did not start until April 1902, by when over £500 had been raised. It was completed by November that year when the Bishop of Oxford presided over a service to re-open the Church. This was impressively fast for such extensive work.

By good chance we have photographic evidence of the work in progress. In 1999 a box of glass photographic plates was found on a market stall in Eastbourne. These included the ones shown in Figure 2.12, which indicate the scale of what was involved.

Figure 2.12: The 1902 restoration in progress

The photo on the left is taken from above the nave, the roof of which has been removed. It shows the top of the chancel arch partially obscured with scaffolding. Two workmen are visible to the right of the picture. The photo on the right is taken from the back of the nave looking east towards the chancel arch. It can be seen that the pews remained in place during the work.

During the work a timber beam was found hidden in the chancel arch. The photograph of it shown in Figure 2.13 is annotated on the back in what appears to be a contemporary hand:

---

[13] The boiler ran on coke that was tipped down a shute from outside into the boiler house under the floor of the Church about halfway down the north side. The hot air came up through grilles in the floor. The underfloor boiler house and the internal end of the shute were revealed during the work to replace the floor in 2008-2009. The boiler house was not filled in and remains in situ under the floor.

Original chancel arch? – found embedded in masonry above sham plaster arch showing some of original interior decoration.

Unfortunately, the decoration is not visible in the photograph.

Figure 2.13: Old chancel beam in the churchyard during the restoration work

The fundraising was a much more drawn out process than the restoration work itself and one which seemed to cause some strain for the vicar, on whom the main burden fell.

The initial appeal was launched in February 1900, with 500 printed leaflets sent out. Further repeat mailings were made in 1902 and 1903. A total of 216 people and organisations subscribed, with some making more than one donation, giving 276 in all. Individual donations ranged upwards to £25, and raised a total of just over £700. Grants from historic churches' funds raised £139. Radley College donated £50 and raised a further £31 through chapel collections. Church collections and the Church box raised £90. A very impressive £450 was raised by fetes, concerts and jumble sales, in which Mrs Josephine Dockar-Drysdale was to the fore. However, the full £1,532 7s 10½d cost of the project was not recovered until the Committee's last meeting on 24 November 1904, and only then by committee members contributing some £22 out of their own pockets for miscellaneous costs such as printing which had been met by the vicar and not hitherto reimbursed.

It is apparent from the correspondence that the vicar disliked the whole process of what he called 'begging', especially when he was met by unsympathetic responses and/or had to make repeat approaches to the same people. Some flavour comes from the correspondence. The vicar wrote to the archdeacon in March or April 1901 saying:

> I have worked hard at begging but alas with <u>very slow</u> results … and where I turn I hardly know. The many appeals I have already sent out have been almost barren of results …

The archdeacon replied rather unsympathetically promising two guineas, which he hedged around with various caveats about the progress of the work. The vicar probably did not think this very generous, but even this sum failed to appear and he was placed in the awkward position of having to write a chasing letter two years later:

> Therefore pardon my writing to remind you for the promise, and to ask if you would kindly send me the same.

In October 1902 he received a welcome promise of money from the trustees of a Mr Kingston's will, only to discover a condition of the will that restricted donations to 'low churchmen'. This caused him to wrestle with his conscience and to write to the trustees that:

> I am not in what in common talk is understood to be a <u>low</u> churchman. I would rather simply call myself an obedient churchman, trying honestly to keep the rubric, and not a member of either extreme party.

Fortunately the trustees were pragmatic and let the appeal have five guineas.

Perhaps the Revd Longland did not always help himself. Blanche Norton, who lived at Braeside (a large house near the Church) wrote to him in June 1904 with the proceeds of a fete which she and Josephine Dockar-Drysdale had organised, and for which the latter had donated prizes. Her letter says rather tartly:

> We regretted that neither you nor Mrs Longland found a few minutes to come round and see them [the prizes] presented.

At the end of the fundraising process, the committee passed a motion expressing:

> their warm appreciation of the untiring energy and patience with which Mr Longland had seen this important and necessary work begin and finished.

Revd Longland must have been very relieved when it was all over, but the benefit to the fabric of the church is unquestionable.

More recent additions and restorations

The Church has continued to be adapted, improved and repaired over the last century.

- A new drainage system was installed in the churchyard in 1907.
- Gas lighting (instead of oil lamps) was introduced in 1926 to be replaced by electric lighting in 1937.
- The screen at the tower's arch and the choir vestry date from 1928.
- The bells were re-hung in 1928 and again in 1952 and 2015.
- The hot air heating system was replaced in 1952 by one using water and radiators, and the external boiler house built. The boiler was converted from solid fuel to oil in 1962, and later to gas.
- In 1963 the balcony above the west end of the nave was constructed, accessed by a spiral staircase donated by Radley College.
- 1963 also saw a major replacement of the roof slates and battens.

Interestingly, a much more fundamental adaptation was planned in 1960 but not implemented. In the belief that there had originally been a north aisle, a project was put in hand to rebuild it. The vicar, Robert Brutton, obtained an informal estimate that this could be achieved at the surprisingly low cost of £2,900. He wrote for support to the bishop, who replied that he could not promise any funding priority. Nevertheless Brutton secured the agreement of Revd Lt Colonel Vivien Seymer of Wimbledon (an old boy of Radley College) to supervise the work and Seymer obtained three tenders. We do not have a record of them, but there is a letter of 30 January 1962 from Seymer to Brutton saying that the tenders must 'have come as a terrible shock' to him. Presumably they were well in excess of the original estimate of £2,900. Quite what then happened is unclear but none of the tenderers was appointed to do the work and the project must have been abandoned. A record of 16 February 1962 of a 'fundraising sub-committee' indicates that little serious consideration had been given to raising the money required.

Most recently a major restoration, based on necessity, was carried out with a very successful fundraising exercise to finance it. This exercise, which has some echoes of the 1902 restoration, is described in the next section.

Death watch beetle restoration of 2008 to 2009

In 2008 a death watch beetle infestation was discovered in the Church. A survey by a diocesan architect, Robert Montgomery, highlighted three crucial problem areas:

- much of the floor of the nave was damaged by beetle, other infestation and rot, and needed repairing or replacing;
- the organ, and the floor on which it stood, had been damaged and needed to be removed, restored and reinstated;
- many of the pews were badly damaged and in need of replacement.

Fortunately the chancel and balcony had not been attacked. As with the 1902 restoration there was an appeal for funds, co-ordinated in this case by the Friends of St James the Great, a committee formed of Revd Pam McKellen (the vicar), Graham Steinsberg, David Handscomb (Parochial Church Council treasurer), Jo McDougall, Emma Moore, Simon Birkett and Judy Harris. This committee approached a number of possible sources of funding and organised a series of fundraising initiatives. Letters seeking support were sent to Church members and delivered to everyone in the village. A grant of £20,000 was received from the Historic Churches Trust, but the great majority of donations came from within the village and events organised by the village – strikingly more so than in 1902 when the village was much smaller and arguably less active. Major fundraising events included:

- a Hide and Seek Art Exhibition at the Sewell Centre, Radley College, in March 2009 which raised over £3,000;
- the 'Imagine the Beatles' concert and auction at the New Theatre, Radley College, on 18 October 2008 which raised £10,000.

The Church was closed for repair from June 2008 until February 2009, during which time services were held in the hall of Radley Church of England Primary School next to the Church. Work included:

- moving out all the old pews;
- taking up the wooden parts of the floor and the wooden pew platforms;
- levelling the floor in the nave and the south transept;
- putting down a stone floor using existing stonework where possible and replacement stone ('hand worn beige limestone') to fill the gaps;
- removing the organ, repairing damage to it and reinstating it;
- providing new seating – a combination of wooden chairs and pews custom made for the Church by Irish Contract Seating;
- installing a new gas-fired boiler and heating system;
- redecorating the interior.

Rayners Contractors Ltd of Abingdon carried out the main building works. The nave was totally cleared for the works. The chancel was used for storage and protected by a polythene dividing curtain. Organ pipes and organ parts not affected were stored locally, while the damaged and more fragile parts were taken to London to the workshops of Bishop & Son for repair. The organ was returned to its original location in the south transept, though positioned slightly further back. The final cost of the repair work was £180,000. Figure 2.14 shows the work in progress.

Figure 2.14: Nave excavation in 2008 as part of the death watch beetle eradication
The photo is taken from near the pulpit looking south-west towards the porch.

The re-opening on Saturday 14 February 2009 was marked by an Open Day, which began with a peal of bells at 10 am. The sunlight streamed through the stained glass windows and the Church appeared full of light. There was a beetle hunt, performances by the choir, prayers and readings. Refreshments were served throughout the day in the Church Room next door to the Church, where there was also an exhibition on the history of the Church by Radley History Club and of photographs taken during the building work. Some 300 people visited the Church to see the new floor, chairs and pews. The chairs and pews feature the St James scallop (see Chapter 3), also seen on the beautiful communion table in matching wood given to the Church.

Looking back on these months, Pam McKellen has some strong and sometimes emotional memories. What could have been a devastating crisis for the Church did much to reinforce the bond between the Church and its wider community. It also transformed the Church into a space that could be much more flexible as a centre of community activity.

Before the death watch beetle was discovered, the vicar and Parochial Church Council had already been considering a reordering[14] – involving relatively minor alterations to remove the front pews to create more flexible space for events such as weddings. At a meeting to discuss this, Robert Montgomery, the diocesan architect, had remarked on some spongy floor near the organ and after lifting a floorboard declared that there was death watch beetle. Perhaps prescient of the opportunity, Pam replied by saying 'thank you'. As the full extent of the infestation became clear she and the Parochial Church Council needed to take decisions about the response:

- patch and mend or a more strategic renewal;
- restore the organ or replace it with a smaller modern electronic one;
- stone or wood floor;
- pews or chairs.

They worked closely on this with the architect and visited other churches in the area. The decision was to keep and restore the organ, renew the floor in stone, and to have a mix of pews and chairs – both to be movable. Care was taken to select the right stone and wood. Pam is very pleased with the result, not just the quality of the materials but the opportunity that movable seating has provided to make much more flexible use of the Church – achieving on a larger scale the kind of change under consideration when the infestation was discovered.

Pam particularly recalls the moving Church services that punctuated the work. At the end of the last service in the Church before the work, a cross, a bible, a chalice and plate, and a small font were ceremonially processed to the School Hall, which was to become the temporary site for services during the closure. On Christmas Day, and before the work was complete, the nave was cleared sufficiently to hold a special service there. And when the work was finally complete, the cross, chalice and other items were ceremonially processed back from the School Hall to the Church, where the first service was held with the new seating on 15 February 2009. A special service was held by the Bishop of Reading, the Rt Revd Stephen Cottrell, on 1 March 2009 to bless and dedicate the reordering of the Church.

Related Church buildings

Alongside the Church is a small group of related buildings (Figure 2.15). To the north is the Vicarage. To the east is Radley Church of England Primary School. Between the Church and the School are the Church Room and a small 'Hut' built for the use of young people in the

---

[14] Changes to the arrangement of the worship space

village. These buildings are described in turn below. The churchyard and the Upper Cemetery are dealt with in Chapter 4.

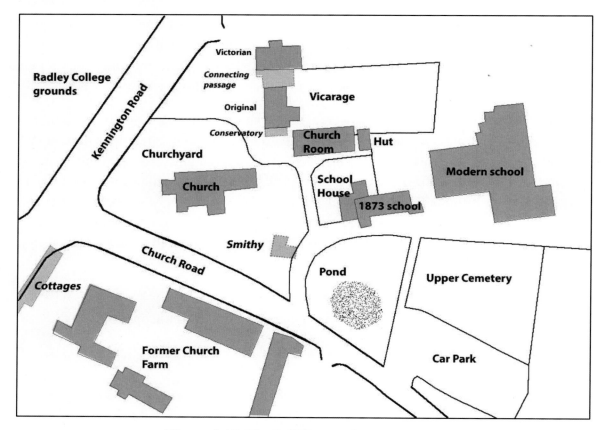

Figure 2.15: The buildings near the Church
The map shows the buildings of today in darker shade. Buildings in existence at the end of the nineteenth century but since demolished are shown in lighter shade with their names in italics.

The Vicarage

The Vicarage is undoubtedly a very fine old building (Figure 2.16) and might well be the oldest building in the country to have been in continuous use as the home of a church's incumbent.[15] But, as indicated below, there have been differing views both about its antiquity and its original use.

In 1952 it was listed by (what is now) Historic England as being originally late fifteenth century, with an early seventeenth century extension. In 2004 a survey was carried out by members of the Radley History Club assisted by experts from Oxfordshire Buildings Record. They agreed with the 1952 listing on the dating of the extension but dated the original structure rather earlier to the thirteenth or fourteenth century.

The only firm documentary evidence dating to medieval times is an Abingdon Abbey record of 1271 referring to a 'house with a croft in which the chaplains serving Radley were accustomed to stay'. The diocesan surveyor, Ernest Ravenscroft, in a report of June 1940 said

---

[15] Alan Savidge, in his book *The Parsonage in England,* has reviewed all the potential candidates for this honour and considers that Radley's claim is a 'very respectable one'.

that the Vicarage was built in 1382, and that it was reputed to be the oldest parsonage in the country, but provided no evidence.

Figure 2.16: Radley Vicarage today

There is also an oft repeated legend that the building was originally not a vicarage at all, but a hunting lodge for the Abbey which was stayed in amongst others by Henry VII. This legend has no known documentary basis. It may have been encouraged by the presence in the church of a stained glass portrait of King Henry VII, but this was a Victorian addition inserted from elsewhere. There may also have been a notion that Radley could not have had a house for its incumbent when it was simply a chaplaincy of St Helen's, but the deed of 1271 shows this to be incorrect.

As ever there is much uncertainty, but there seems little reason to doubt the origins of the building as a vicarage – or more strictly a chaplain's house. We know from the Abbey's document of 1271 that the chaplains did indeed have a house in Radley and the location of the Vicarage is just where one would expect to find it. It might be that the 1271 house was an earlier one, later replaced, but even if that were the case we seem to have a medieval home for Radley's incumbent, which has probably been used as such right from then to the present day.

We know from Hearth Tax records in the 1660s that the building had five fireplaces, making it one of the most comfortable in the village. It is also recorded in an inventory of 1669 as having 'several' rooms and it seems likely that the building had been extended by then.

Figures 2.17 and 2.18, which distinguish between the original structure and the seventeenth century extension, show the west elevation and ground plan of the building respectively.

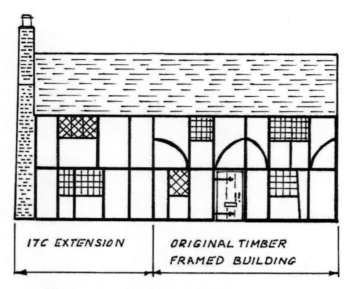

Figure 2.17: West elevation of the Vicarage

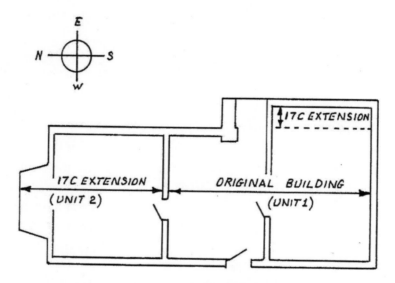

Figure 2.18: Ground plan of the Vicarage

Since then the main change was the addition in 1869 of a brick-built building to the north linked by a corridor, making a very substantial home. This was very much the initiative of Radley College which met the £500 cost. While the new building provided the vicar with extra space, it was for most of the time shared with wider College uses, especially as an overflow dormitory, rather than being part of the vicar's private home – which remained in the old building. During the period 1893 to 1898, the new building also provided housing for the Community of the Resurrection, who were at that time based in Radley (see Chapter 5).

A conservatory was added to the south of the old building and the photograph in Figure 2.19, taken around the turn of the century, shows that the Vicarage was a very agreeable one. On the left is the Victorian building and connecting corridor. The conservatory is just visible on the right.

Figure 2.19: Vicarage from the west around 1900

Rather greater change, however, might easily have occurred in the 1940s. In 1939, when Ernest Ravenscroft surveyed the building prior to it being occupied by the new incumbent, Eustace Heriz-Smith, he found major structural problems, with walls bulging and the roof spreading, and doubted whether the cost of repair could be justified. He recommended that consideration be given to demolition with replacement by a smaller building or merging Radley parish with Kennington.

The Council of Radley College, as patron, was not happy with these options and commissioned a survey by the Society for Preservation of Ancient Buildings, which considered the building to be basically sound. The Society recommended relatively minor repairs at a cost of £200 and a new extension at a cost of £450. Radley College did not believe the extension could be justified but supported the repairs, sharing the cost with the Ecclesiastical Commissioners.

These repairs clearly did not solve the problem. In June 1940 the Oxford Diocese Dilapidation Board reported that 'the experiences of the last winter have convinced the incumbent (Heriz-Smith) that it is impossible to face another winter under these conditions'. Quite what action followed is unclear, but the Board had suggested reducing the level of the surrounding ground and introducing central heating, and it might be that this was done.

The next we hear is in 1949 by when John Pixell is the vicar. While on holiday in July he learnt by letter that part of the ceiling had collapsed and that Radley College had undertaken urgent work to avert 'imminent catastrophe'. Ernest Ravenscroft carried out a fresh survey, doubtless bemoaning the fact that his previous recommendations had been over-ruled. His recommendations were similar, but even more extensive including replacement rather than repair of the roof timbers. Radley College seemed this time to accept the need for major repair work as did the Oxford Diocese Dilapidations Board, but Pixell was advised to approach Walter Godfrey, an architect of Steventon, for a second opinion …

…and an opinion he certainly got! Godfrey wrote as follows:

> The report [by Ernest Ravenscroft] is obviously written by someone quite unacquainted with buildings of the age of Radley Vicarage … and its conclusions are vitiated by being based on the quite irrelevant point of view of modern times. If all our ancient buildings … were condemned on similar fictitious grounds we should lose most of our wonderful built heritage.

Like the Society for Preservation of Ancient Buildings, Godfrey argued that the structure was sound, that the building was dry, and that only minor repair was needed.

How this was resolved is unclear, but the Vicarage does seem to have become a more agreeable place in which to live. Between 1971 and 1988 when Daniel Pope was vicar, his daughter Judy Harris has memories of the Vicarage being a comfortable home with central heating and secondary glazing to keep it warm. It was also a spacious place, in which domestic, pastoral and Radley College uses were shared.

The domestic living area was principally the old medieval building, but the kitchen and everyday eating area was in the corridor between it and the Victorian building. The downstairs rooms in the latter were used for family gatherings, meetings and events such as wedding and christening receptions. Its upstairs rooms were used as a dormitory for four or so Radley College boys and for putting up College guests.

This mix of uses came to an end when a major restoration was carried out by the Diocese in 1989 to 1990. At this time the parish of Radley was merged with the parish of Sunningwell to create a unified benefice (see Chapter 1) with Keith Kinnaird, the vicar of Sunningwell, taking on Radley as well (see Chapter 5).

The Diocese reviewed the future of the Vicarage as its renovation could be justified only if the vicar of the United Benefice was to move there. Before his appointment Keith Kinnaird confirmed that he would like to make it his family home and the work proceeded.

The work was undertaken by the Diocese, whose role this now was, rather than Radley College. The corridor to the Victorian building to the north was demolished (see Figure 2.20) and the Vicarage returned to its detached and self-sufficient origins – a single medieval building containing all it needed and not sharing space with the College.

The now detached Victorian building is today called Gore House and is used by the College for staff accommodation. It is named after Charles Gore, the former vicar who was a founder of the Community of the Resurrection.

Figure 2.20: The Vicarage from the rear (east) during restoration works of 1989 to 1990
On the left is the old medieval building where a rear extension has been demolished
prior to construction of a new kitchen extension. On the right is the Victorian
building. The connecting corridor in between is in the process of demolition.

A new kitchen was constructed at the back of the medieval building to replace the one lost in the demolished linking corridor. Externally the trellising had already been removed and the walls were re-roughcast. The conservatory to the south had by now also been demolished.

Some features of the old building were lost and Judy Harris bemoans the removal of an old brick floor. The exterior (Figure 2.21) is much less cottagey and a little bleak, but conveys a more authentic feel of its age.

Viewed from the safety of the twenty-first century, it is difficult to sympathise either with Ravenscroft's proposals for demolition/major repair or with his conservationist critics, who seemed distanced from the reality of maintaining and living in the building.

The current vicar, Pam McKellen, appreciates the decisions which have retained the building as a vicarage, marrying reasonable modern comfort with clearly visible medieval character. She is not taken in by stories of vicarage ghosts, but does feel the privilege of living in the house from which men and now women of the cloth have served the local Radley community more or less continuously for over 600 years.

Pam is retiring just as this book is being published and her hope is that the building will continue to be the home of her successors as vicar.

Figure 2.21: The Vicarage from the front (west) following the restoration of 1989 to 1990

The Primary School

Radley Church of England Primary School is the subject of a book in its own right published in 2008 by Radley History Club. This chapter therefore limits itself to the main points in the history of its buildings.

The early origins of the school are uncertain, but there was a village school with its own building by the time of the 1852 religious census and there appears to have been a Sunday school as early as 1807. The relationship between the two is uncertain and it may well be that one evolved into the other. What is clearer is that the school building was unsatisfactory, with highly adverse reports from HM Inspector of Schools in 1866 and 1867. The heating seemed to have been particularly inadequate and at times was non-existent. Interestingly, the Inspector also commented adversely on the location of the school, close to the Church but not to the area of the village (what is now Lower Radley) where most of the children lived.

In 1872 a new replacement school was constructed. This was opened in January 1873 and still exists as the old Victorian part of the current school. The building was on land leased from Sir George Bowyer whose family owned most of the village at that time (see Chapter 1). The lease was vested in the vicar and churchwardens, and required the school to promote the education of the poor in the principles of the Church of England. Although the school paid a rent of £1 6s 0d, this was more than covered by an annual donation of £5 made to the school by the Bowyers.

In 1897 Miss Mary Bowyer, Sir George's sister who by now owned the land, donated it to the vicar and churchwardens, along with an adjoining parcel on which the smithy was sited. This latter parcel of land allowed the graveyard to be extended (see Chapter 4), while the former provided future security for the school. The conveyance caused some later concern because it was not made explicit that the school was to be a denominational church school, raising potential doubt about its status and funding. Lawyers advised, however, that these concerns were not sufficiently founded and it has always been accepted that the school is a Church of England primary school. The land is now vested in the School House Land Trust.

It is interesting that the new 1873 school building was sited very much as before, not near where people lived in Lower Radley, despite the Inspector's concerns on that point. Perhaps this was prescient as the centre of population has since moved to the upper village. The building, although an improvement on the one before, proved troublesome with issues about drainage, sanitation and heating. As the village grew after the Second World War extra capacity was also needed. A new classroom block was built in 1957, with further extensions in 1963, 1969 and 2008. The school now has around 130 pupils and there is renewed discussion about its further extension or rebuilding to accommodate children from proposed additional housing in the village.

Church Room

When Dan Pope became vicar in 1971, there was a parish room adjoining the vicarage, but it was in a very poor state and he called a parish meeting to discuss its future. It was agreed that it was beyond practical repair and that a new freestanding building should be constructed. This became a major project of his incumbency. The new building was finally opened and blessed by the Bishop of Reading, the Rt Revd Eric Wild, in August 1983. Since then it has been used very successfully by the Church, the Parish Council and a wide variety of community organisations. The income from non-church use has helped fund new projects.

The building of the new Church Room (Figure 2.22), with attached store, was very much a community project. The construction was put out to tender at a cost of some £35,000, but much of the labour and materials was provided free by the congregation and local donors. For instance, the Radley-based company J. Curtis & Sons provided the aggregates, a local brewery provided the furniture and Radley Women's Institute provided the curtains. The old parish room was demolished by parishioners and the electrics were fitted by a local electrician, Peter Hockham, who is commemorated as a 'bright spark' by a plaque in the churchyard. At the opening ceremony, the vicar particularly recognised the 'unstinting services' of Derek Turrill, 'the right man in the right place at the right time'.

Fundraising activities included a 50:50 auction at Radley College and concerts organised by the Church's entertainments committee. A shortfall at the end was made up by a legacy from a parishioner.

The Church Room has since been repainted and in 2015-16 was given a more significant uplift with new flooring, a disabled toilet, new stackable chairs and new folding tables.

Figure 2.22: The Church Room

The School House and the Hut

Adjoining the Victorian school building is the School House (Figure 2.23). This predated the 1873 school but its precise age is uncertain. The School House became the home of the head teachers up until the retirement of Miss Cross in 1974. It was then let as a private dwelling. The freehold is vested in the School House Land Trust. The house yields a rent of about £5,000 a year, which can be put to the Trust's charitable purposes. For example, the income was used to landscape the school's grounds following the 2008 extension and in 2014 to construct a 'Hut' to be used by the school and youth groups. The Hut belies its name and is a very solid wooden structure, with disabled access and heating, erected at a cost of around £40,000 by Wentworth Garden Rooms. It is beside the Church Room taking in what was part of the Vicarage garden. Users include the Church youth group and the village Kids' Club.

Figure 2.23: The School House

Sources

General accounts of the history and features of the church buildings can be found in:

- *Radley, Ancient Barrows to Modern Parish*, P. Drysdale, 1985
- *The History of Radley*, P. Drysdale, R. Ford, P. Groser, M. Orchard, A. Parkes and K. Williams, 2002
- *Radley Church and Parish*, S. Allso, 1971
- *Radley Church and Parish: A Brief History*, Radley History Club, 2009
- *The Buildings of England: Berkshire*, G. Tyack, S. Bradley and N. Pevsner, Pevsner Architecture Guides, 2010
- *History of Berkshire, Vol. 4*, Victoria County History (VCH), 1924, pp. 410-416

Additionally the following sources have been consulted on particular aspects of this chapter.

Early origins

The Deserted Medieval Villages of North Berkshire, J. Brooks, unpublished PhD thesis, University of Reading, 1982

The Two Cartularies of Abingdon, G. Lambrick and C.F. Slade, Volume 2, Oxford History Society New Series XXXIII, 1990

Civil War, aisle and transept

Abingdon 1556-1702, Peace and War: The Story of Abingdon Part III, M. Cox, 1993

Abingdon at War, 1642-1646, Abingdon Area Archaeological and Historical Society website, www.abingdon.gov.uk/feature-articles/abingdon-war-1642-1646

Cropredy Bridge, 1644: The Campaign and the Battle, M. Toynbee and P. Young, 1970

Radley Church, Abingdon Archaeological Geophysics, Short Report Form No. 2014-15

The Civil War in Oxfordshire, D. Eddershaw, 1995

The Life and Times of Anthony Wood, antiquary of Oxford, Vol 1 1632-1665, A. Clark (ed.), 1891

The Rebuilding and Repair of Berkshire Churches during the Seventeenth, Eighteenth and Nineteenth Centuries, B. Clarke and H. Colvin, 1952

Churchwardens' Presentments, Berkshire Record Office, D/A2/C.129

The architectural evidence is based inter alia on observation by, and discussion with, David Clark, FSA, secretary of the Oxfordshire Buildings Record. Professor Bob Evans, Manfred Brod and Stephen Barker were consulted on the historical evidence.

Anglo-Catholic plans of 1895

The drawings are in the Berkshire Record Office at D/P95/6/4.

Restoration of 1902

Detailed specifications, minute books, accounts and correspondence can be found in the Berkshire Record Office, mainly under the following references:

D/P95/6/1
D/P95/6/5
D/P95/6/6
D/P95/6/7
D/P95/6/8

More recent additions and restorations

Records in the Berkshire Record Office are less complete than for the 1902 restoration but can be found under the following references:

D/P95/6/1
D/P95/6/2
D/P95/6/9
D/P95/6/10

Death watch beetle restoration of 2008 to 2009

Radley Village website, www.radleyvillage.org.uk

Interview with Revd Pam McKellen, 19 October 2015

Related Church buildings

Radley Vicarage, Radley History Club, 2005

The History of Radley CE Primary School, Christine Wootton, 2008

The Parsonage in England: Its History and Architecture, Alan Savidge, 1964

Records of surveys and correspondence relating to the Vicarage (especially 1939 to 1941 and 1949) can be found in the Berkshire Record Office, mainly under the following references:

D/P95/3/1
D/P95/3/6

Interviews with:

Judy Harris, 9 February 2015

Keith Kinnaird, 17 August 2015

Revd Pam McKellen, 19 October 2015

Derek Turrill, 2 July 2015

Photographs courtesy of Brian Ford, Les Hemsworth, John Huddleston, Keith Kinnaird, Pam McKellen and Radley History Club archives

Chapter 3: The Interior of Radley Church

by Felicity Henderson

Radley Church, dedicated to St James the Great, has seen the gathering together of village people to celebrate baptisms and marriages, and to mourn the death of loved ones, for more than 700 years. The interior of the Church today is light and airy, loved and cared for by its congregation, and still the scene of many family gatherings for baptisms, weddings and funerals, as well as being the place where a sizeable congregation meets for worship Sunday by Sunday.

Step inside Radley Church to 700 years of history

Inside the Church there is evidence of many changes to the building over the centuries. The building we see today dates from about 1290 onwards, but much of it has been obscured by various renovations over the centuries, including the complete restoration in 1902 (see Chapter 2). In addition, evidence of an even earlier church remains, often well hidden. Most recently, the Church was reordered[1] following the discovery of death watch beetle in 2008.

The interior of Radley Church testifies to the involvement of many people over the centuries. Not only abbots and bishops, clergy and churchwardens, lords and landowners, craftsmen and builders but also ordinary village people – unknown to us but known in their own time and within their own community, many of them buried in the churchyard (see Chapter 4).

The history of Radley Church can best be seen in a tour of the building. Very little remains of the earliest structure, possibly Saxon or early Norman, which is presumed to have existed until, it is said, it burned down towards the end of the thirteenth century. But a history of the Church must start with the front door!

Entering the Church building

The Church is entered through the south porch (see plan overleaf). This is of Victorian origin, but the large oak door probably dates from the sixteenth century. On the outside is carved 'Rodericus Lloid 1606' (see Chapter 5). He was the vicar between *c*.1602 and *c*.1613. One assumes it was acceptable for the vicar to write his own name on the church door, rather than imagine this was done by a naughty choirboy on a rainy afternoon.

On this door there appear to be two handles: the lower one is not strictly a handle but the sanctuary ring or knocker. This could be used by anyone wishing to claim the ancient right of sanctuary within the building, until they could lawfully be brought to trial. There is no record of any one seeking sanctuary in Radley Church, but rings such as this one date back to the earliest Christian churches in Europe.

---

[1] To reorder a church is to rearrange or adapt the existing building and/or fixtures (for example, removing fixed pews to allow more flexible use of the space).

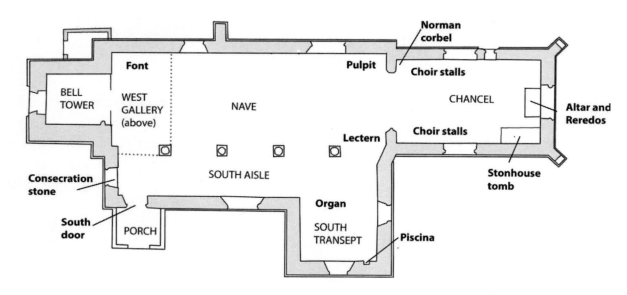

Plan of Radley Church

According to the Berkshire volume of the Victoria County History, the bell tower is 8 ft. 9 in. square, the chancel is 26 ft. 6 in. by 14 ft. 6 in. and the nave is 48 ft. 6 in. by 17 ft. 3 in. The south aisle and south transept have a combined width of 26 ft. 9 in. The Church is therefore about 84 ft. (25.5 metres) long and about 44 ft. (13.4 metres) at its widest.

South door detail – the sanctuary ring is below

The font

As you stand on the threshold, the first thing you will see is the Norman font, still in use today for baptising babies in the parish – a fine carved circular bowl for holding the water for baptism. The Norman period is generally taken to be between 1066 and the late twelfth century and we can be almost certain that this font belonged to the church built in Radley which preceded the present building.

The bowl is decorated with an arcade of semi-circular arches, with four carved pillars holding it up, typical of a Norman font. The website of The Corpus of Romanesque Sculpture in Britain & Ireland describes the font as 'one of the most elaborate in the county' and gives the opinion that it dates from the 1170s.

The Norman font

In 1840 the font was discovered buried in the yard of Church Farm opposite. No one knows how it got there, but it is widely assumed that, during the Civil War, it was taken out and buried for safekeeping from Cromwell's troops and then forgotten about. The Latin inscription around the base stone tells of its restoration. The translation reads:

> John Radcliffe, Vicar of this church, [in] AD1840 arranged for [this] most ancient sacred vessel, neglected for a long time at a farm in the district, to be at last preserved again amongst the sacred property.

Another slightly later feature than the font is the consecration stone, set up on the window sill to the left of the entrance just inside the building. Sadly, time and whitewash have taken their toll, but it carries the inscription 'NSM', thought to refer to the bishop who performed the consecration ceremony, Nicolas Longspée, Bishop of Salisbury (then known as Sarum) between 1292 and 1297. It would originally have been placed near the chancel arch.

On the wall behind the font is a map embroidered by members of Radley Women's Institute for the 'Green and Pleasant Land' exhibition organised by the Berkshire Federation of Women's Institutes in Reading in the summer of 1971.

The nave

As you turn to your right into the nave, one of the building's most striking features is the presence of large oak pillars making an arcade between the nave and the south aisle, and holding up the roof.

The south arcade

The wooden pillars are unusual and unexpected; in almost all churches in England the pillars are made of stone. The few churches that do have wooden pillars are mostly in Shropshire and Cheshire.

These four huge tree trunks, on stone bases, reputedly have an interesting origin: it is said that the abbot of Abingdon responsible for building the nave was told in a dream to 'seek pillars in the forest'. The nave roof itself is also held up by wooden arches. As a plaque on the north wall tells us, the arches which we see today were presented by Mrs Josephine Dockar-Drysdale, as a memorial to her father, William Dockar, and were installed as part of the 1902 restoration work (see Chapter 2).

Left: The nave today. Right: An older photograph showing the wooden pillars and south aisle

The limestone floor of the nave, and the light oak pews and chairs, are evidence of the reordering work in 2008 to 2009 following an infestation of death watch beetle (see Chapter 2). The chairs bear the sign of St James the Great. The scallop shell, his symbol, has been linked to the shrine of St James at Santiago de Compostela in Spain, a place of pilgrimage from the eleventh or twelfth century right up to the present day. In his fourteenth century *Canterbury Tales*, Chaucer describes the Wife of Bath wearing the scallop shell and comments on her extensive travels.

The scallop shell – the symbol of St James the Great

All the new oak pews are moveable, allowing flexible use of the space for events as needed.

The Church cleared ready to welcome those making the Lantern Walk from Peach Croft Farm to the Church on 22 December 2015

It could be said that the reordering restored the Church to its original format: we do not know when pews were first installed in Radley Church, but typically they were introduced in churches after the Reformation of the sixteenth century, when preaching and Bible reading became much more important in church life. Before that, people stood up during the service, and the old and infirm sat on ledges or benches around the walls. Once there were pews, people would have been expected to sit down to listen to the sermons (possibly rather long ones) and Bible readings, rather than stand or move about.

There would also have been another very visible difference in pre-Reformation times. Instead of the whitewashed walls, the interior would have been brightly coloured and decorated with wall paintings. These would have brought to life in pictures the stories of the Bible for an illiterate congregation, few of whom would have understood the Latin services. Sadly, we do not have any remains of pre-existing wall paintings in Radley Church, or any other medieval features that were common to all churches such as a rood screen between the nave and the chancel. We know that, under Elizabeth I, it was mandatory to whitewash over medieval wall paintings and that, in 1561, all parish churches were instructed to display the Ten Commandments and other scriptures (in English) on the wall of the east end of the church. This underlines the new emphasis on reading and words that characterised the Reformation and Protestant practice. However, we have no evidence of this in Radley either.

Up until the sixteenth century, like all churches in England, Radley would have been a Catholic church. The Reformation of the English church was influenced both by the politically motivated break away from the Church of Rome by Henry VIII and by the waves of Protestant reforms across much of northern Europe. This was the first time that ordinary people were able to hear the words of the Bible in English, not Latin. The Book of Common Prayer was first published in 1549 and much later in 1662 revised in the well-known format still used for some services in churches today. Having gone through a number of revisions, the translation of the whole Bible into English approved for use in English churches, was eventually published in 1611 as the King James Bible, also known as the Authorised Version.

Moving up the nave, we come to the crossing, where the east–west and north–south arms of a church meet. A portable nave altar had been used for certain services for a number of years but a new, moveable nave altar was consecrated with the new floor, pews and chairs after the death watch beetle reordering. The wood and decoration of this specially commissioned altar match those of the pews and chairs. It is moved into the crossing for use at Communion services except those on the third Sunday of each month.

The lectern

To the right of the crossing as you look at the high altar is the lectern, in the form of a large wooden eagle with wings outstretched, dating from the nineteenth century. Typical of many churches in England, this holds the large Bible which is to be read aloud to the congregation. The eagle, traditionally the symbol of St John, the Gospel writer, can be taken to represent the way God's 'word' is flying out into the world.

The pulpit and canopy

To the left of the crossing is the pulpit, from which the congregation is addressed for the sermon or talk. The pulpit is not ancient; although stone and decorated in the Tudor style, it probably dates from the late nineteenth century.

The rather grand carved wooden canopy over the pulpit is famously said to have been the canopy over the Speaker's chair in Parliament, given in 1653 to the Church by William Lenthall, a local man and Speaker of the House of Commons through the turbulent years of the Long Parliament until forced to leave by Cromwell. Despite extensive research, there is no way of verifying this story, and although Lenthall was from Besselsleigh, only a few miles away, there is nothing to link him to Radley Church. Another version is that the canopy was on its way from London via the Thames to Burford Priory, which Lenthall was restoring for himself, and was somehow intercepted at Radley or Abingdon. However, in a letter of 20 February 1900 from Edward Barber (Radley curate 1868-1883) to Charles Longland (vicar 1898-1916), seemingly in reply to an enquiry from the latter about the pulpit, Barber said he had always assumed Sir George Bowyer (1810-1883) had acquired and installed the canopy. More recently, it has been suggested that the carved panelling and canopy may have originated in Abingdon Abbey, being reused following the dissolution. At this point, we can only say that its origins remain uncertain.

The pulpit with canopy above

The north wall of the nave

The windows in the north wall date from the fifteenth century; the stained glass is discussed later in this chapter. While Radley has a south aisle and transept, the existence of a north aisle and transept is heavily debated (see Chapter 2).

On the north wall of the nave are two items of interest. The first is a brass plaque, a village war memorial dedicated to those who died in the two world wars (eight from 1914-1918 and five from 1939-1945) – their names familiar to generations of Radley people. The second is a large diamond-shaped funeral hatchment in memory of Sir George Bowyer (1783-1860). It is made of wood and features the coats of arms of Sir George himself, his wife and their forebears, including the Stonhouse family. Funeral hatchments originally stood outside the home of the deceased for quite a while after the burial and only later were brought into the church. Sir George is buried in the family vault (see Chapter 4).

The stained glass windows

There has been uncertainty concerning the origins and date of the very fine stained glass windows, which show representations of the Royal Arms of the Plantagenet and Tudor kings (subjects from the fifteenth and sixteenth centuries) and three examples of continental stained glass (the 'lights' to left and right of the east window, and the centre light on the north nave window). These magnificent windows seem quite surprising for a small village church, but although there are as yet no known records of any pre-existing stained glass, it is known that the heraldic stained glass was a gift in about 1840 from a patron, George Bowyer (1810-1883), son and heir to the Sir George Bowyer whose funeral hatchment is on the north wall. It used to be thought that the continental stained glass was given by the Revd William Sewell, one of the founders of Radley College, but it is now thought that this too was a gift from George Bowyer, who went on to donate the choir stalls in 1847 (see below).

Stained glass: Henry VII, in the west window (bell tower)

The heraldic stained glass is known to be by the famous Thomas Willement (1786-1871), who started his career studying heraldry and later became 'artist in stained glass' to Queen Victoria. Willement is described by local historian, Patrick Drysdale, as 'an active participant in the Gothic Revival'. He installed similar glass at many other churches and colleges including St George's Chapel, Windsor, and several Oxford colleges. Radley College is also thought to contain examples of Willement's work.

Over the years there has been considerable discussion about how much of the stained glass was of medieval origin and restored by Willement, and how much was Willement's own work. The verdict seems to be that it is all Willement's work. For a much fuller and very well researched account of this argument, see *Faith and Heraldry* by Patrick Drysdale, to whom I am indebted for this section of the chapter.

The chancel

Continuing our tour of the Church, we move into the chancel. The arch is part of the restoration of 1902. However, tucked behind and to the right of the arch, facing the west end of the Church, is another clue to the origins of Radley Church. Here is a small stone Norman corbel (a sort of projecting bracket for holding up masonry such as an arch or a beam). Like the consecration stone by the entrance, this has been painted over and is difficult to see, but it suggests that some of the earlier church was incorporated during the rebuilding at the end of the thirteenth century.

As in much of the Church, the influence of the patron and local landowner is evident – the Stonhouses and then the Bowyers who followed them as lords of the Manor (see Chapter 1).

The chancel the evening before a wedding
The table and chair are set ready for the signing of the register.

The choir stalls

The choir stalls

The choir stalls, with their delightful misericords featuring cherubic heads on the underside of the seats, date from the 1600s and come from Cologne. They were given to the Church in 1847 by George Bowyer, later Sir George. The misericord, a well-known feature in medieval church choir stalls, is a small ledge on the underside of a seat, which when tipped up allows the occupant to rest while still standing up. One can imagine a weary chorister glad to be able to lean back and perch on his misericord during long and possibly tedious services! The delicately carved canopy over the stalls is possibly a surprising feature to find in a small village church.

A misericord with carving

The altar and reredos

The stone altar is said to be ancient, but is thought to have been refaced in about 1790.

Behind the altar is an elaborate carved and painted reredos, which shows strongly the influence of the Oxford Movement of the nineteenth century. It was installed in 1910, and presented in memory of Arthur Malim, a clergyman who was the priest-in-charge in Radley between 1886 and 1887 (see Chapter 5). The reredos was given by his widow Jane, née Dandridge, who was from an East Hendred family but whose brothers farmed Northcourt Farm in Abingdon. She was also related by marriage to the Badcocks of Wick Farm in Radley. Arthur Malim married Jane at Radley in 1888, even though by that time he is recorded as living in Stowe, Northamptonshire. He was 45 and she was 46: neither of them had been married before. Arthur Malim died in 1892, his widow in 1913. The date of 1910 suggests that Jane Malim was nearly 70 when she presented the reredos to the Church. We do not know what impelled her to give such a generous gift. One way of interpreting this gesture is to surmise that Jane wanted to give thanks for the unexpected happiness of marriage in middle age, her time in Radley warmly and gratefully remembered many years later.

The reredos of 1910 is said to be from the Warham Guild school of church ornament. This linked directly with the Oxford Movement, a period in church history beginning in the second half of the nineteenth century which sought to regain the 'lost' medieval beauty of church liturgy and ornament. However, the Warham Guild was formed in 1912, so the attribution is questionable, though it is recognisably part of the same trend. Another source suggests that the reredos was made by Brother Geldart of The Guild of St Alban the Martyr, a similar guild inspired by John Henry Newman, mostly working with the poor in cities.

The reredos

Designed in the 'Gothic Revival' style, the reredos comprises three sculpted and painted panels: the centre shows the child Christ in glory; the north side portrays St James the Great and the south side St Frideswide, the patron saint of Oxford. This choice of subjects indicates that the reredos was commissioned specifically for Radley. Originally there were two carved gilded angels, one on each side and about 20 inches (50 cm) high at the front corners of the reredos pillars. These were removed in the 1970s to make the chancel lighter and have since been lost. Sadly, the reredos obscures the fine east window showing the arms of Henry VII, echoing the portrait of the same king in the tower window.

The Stonhouse tomb

The memorials in the chancel, as in many churches, are dedicated to the lords of the Manor – in this case, the Stonhouse and Bowyer families, who were patrons and benefactors of the Church over many years.

To the right of the altar is the impressive marble and alabaster Stonhouse family tomb, made to the memory of Sir William Stonhouse, first Baronet of Radley, and to his son Sir John. Sir William died in 1631/2 and his son, John, died unmarried aged 31 later the same year. The first Stonhouse in Radley, William's father George, had purchased the Manor of Radley from Elizabeth I. More about the Stonhouse family and its involvement with Radley can be found in Chapter 1.

The chest tomb is by Nicholas Stone – one of the best sculptors of the time, appointed Master Mason to the Crown, first to James I and then to Charles I in 1626. Stone is famous for his sculpture of John Donne in St Paul's Cathedral in London. The choice of Stone to carve the monument indicates the degree of power, wealth and influence Sir William held, and possibly points to a close connection with King Charles I.

Sir William and his wife, Elizabeth, lie side by side, with their children below, their son John kneeling in prayer on the right, a skull on his knee, the 'memento mori' for all who gaze upon it. In contrast to the skull, a recurring symbol of death in seventeenth century art and poetry, the figures are lifelike, their appearance easily identifying their origins in the Jacobean period. Each wears an intricate ruff and highly decorated costume, indicating high status. In addition, Sir William and Lady Stonhouse rest their heads on representations of luxurious pillows, decorated at the corners with full, flowing tassels. The colours are rich and deep – dark red and green and gold.

The inscription above the tomb is in Latin – a translation can be found beside the tomb. The writer notes that Sir William was 'highly praised for his character, bountiful to the needy and hospitable to the rest' (translated from the Latin). This type of eulogy became popular in the post-Reformation period, when the good character and achievements of the deceased are frequently portrayed and commented on.

One of the most poignant features of the tomb is the representation of the children on the front of the chest tomb: those who died at birth or did not survive infancy are represented as little babies swaddled in their grave clothes.

The Stonhouse tomb

Memorial tablets in the chancel

On the north wall of the chancel are more memorials to both Stonhouses and Bowyers. The Bowyer family inherited the Radley estate when the direct line of the Stonhouse family died out in 1795 (see Chapter 1). Again, we see the portrayal of power and success of the ruling family, not least in the choice of sculptor. There is a memorial to Admiral Sir George Bowyer who died in 1800 aged 60 – a garlanded tablet telling us of his bravery, but how he had to retire from active service following the loss of a leg during a naval battle in 1794 (see Chapter 1). The tablet has an impressively carved flag and symbols of the nautical life (compass, cannon, anchor). We learn that after his injury he 'devoted himself to the quiet occupation of a magistrate and to the exercise of every private virtue'. The carving is signed F. Nollekens – one of the most famous sculptors of his time, known for his busts of George III, William Pitt the Younger, and many other notable and famous people. Next to Admiral Bowyer's memorial is a tablet which commemorates the life of his son, William, described as a Lieutenant Colonel, who died in Barbados, aged only 23, in 1808.

On both sides of the chancel, as in the nave and outside in the churchyard, are yet more reminders that death comes to all – male and female, rich and poor, powerful and powerless.

The Stonhouse and Bowyer families live on in their memorials and the many heraldic shields which remind us of their lineage.

The south transept and aisle

Coming back into the nave, we see the south transept, half hidden by the organ. C. Oldrid Scott, the architect responsible for the 1902 restoration, described the south transept as being 'the untouched work of the fourteenth century' and it is thought to be the oldest part of the Church.

The piscina

The small south transept hides something dating from the beginning of the thirteenth century: on the south wall of the transept are the remains of a small piscina – a small bowl built into the wall of a church, containing water for washing communion vessels.

The organ

The organ, which has two manuals and 15 stops, has an interesting history. A plaque tells us it is dedicated in memory to Dr Edwin George Monk, a man who had some significant influence on Victorian church music. He was not only responsible for establishing the choral tradition of the newly founded Radley College (he was precentor there from 1848 to 1858), but also went on to be organist and master of the choristers at York Minster. He also edited various Anglican music collections as well as composing chants for psalms. In his later years he returned to Radley, living in East Cottage (a semi-detached villa, now 75 Foxborough Road) until he died in 1900. As a result of an appeal for £200 following his death, a new organ was installed by W.J. Fisher of Oxford and dedicated on 3 July 1903 in his memory. Since then it has been overhauled and refurbished in 1925 and 1952, and had a major rebuild in 1982, an overhaul in 2003, and dismantling and repositioning following the reordering in 2008.

Another plaque states that the organ was rebuilt in 1982 by J. Bishop & Son of Ipswich, and also tells us that the 'pipework for the Swell Mixture and Contra Oboe was given by Radley College from the former College Chapel organ, dismantled in 1978'.

It is interesting to note that on the plaque commemorating Dr Monk, there is a reference to one of his other passions – he was a Fellow of the Royal Astronomical Society. Another plaque remembers David Beckett, Organist and Choirmaster from 1972 to 2014.

The history of village churches suggests there would have been an organ in the Church at least since the middle of the nineteenth century. We do not know quite when Radley's first organ was installed, but we know from a contemporary reference that there was definitely one by 1883.

The Revd George Wharton, a curate at Radley between 1876 and 1883 (see Chapter 5), was an organist. Wharton was precentor at Radley College from 1862 to 1914 during which time he notably oversaw the installation of a new organ in the chapel there. He was influential in the installation of the organ in the Church in 1903 and gave a recital at its inauguration.

The organ, dedicated in memory of Dr Edwin Monk
It is considered a good, serviceable organ of reasonable quality.

Memorials and bequests on the south wall

Walking down from the organ, the first memorial tablets on the south wall remember the Davis family – John Davis (died 1820), his brother William (died 1822), William's wife (died 1862, aged 75) and their son John Lawrence (died aged 19 in 1838). John Davis left money to the Church to be used for charitable purposes; the wooden plaque further along the wall contains extracts from his will. The details of this bequest are discussed in Chapter 6 which deals with various financial matters associated with the Church.

Next is a memorial to Revd John Radcliffe, vicar of Radley for more than 40 years (see Chapter 5). The memorial tablet notes 'he died with his prayer book in his hand; on 21 February 1852'. Buried with him is his unmarried sister, Mary, who died 24 years earlier.

Lastly, there is another wooden board, detailing extracts from the will of Martha Bristow, originally from Pumney (or Pomney) Farm. Details of this bequest and more about the family are given in Chapter 6.

The history of the west gallery

The present gallery at the tower end of the Church dates from 1963 when more space was needed for a growing congregation. It is accessed by a small iron spiral staircase given by Radley College. By this staircase is a wooden board listing all the Radley men who served in the First World War.

But during research for this book, we find something very interesting: the churchwardens' records tell us there was an earlier gallery, erected in 1801.

The gallery of 1801

So, what are we to make of this gallery of 1801? Recent interest in the history of church music in rural locations has identified a tradition known as West Gallery music, starting from about the 1720s, but which almost completely disappeared by the mid nineteenth century. In this period, many churches had a west gallery, and there are still surviving examples in Oxfordshire and Berkshire – for example in Ardley near Bicester (installed 1834) and in Berrick Salome near Wallingford (installed 1676). St Nicolas' Church in Abingdon had a west gallery until its 1880 restoration. In this tradition, the singers and musicians, drawn from local people, and often taught by a singing master, would lead the singing in the church from the west gallery – psalms and canticles and later hymns, often sung to locally written tunes. It was also the type of music favoured by dissenters (members of non-conformist churches), such as Methodists. And often the village church 'band' could be heard 'practising' at the village pub. The 'traditional' robed choir processing down the nave to the sound of organ music may be what many of us associate with a village church. But this 'tradition', although performed for many centuries in cathedrals and big city churches, was only adopted in village churches during the second half of the nineteenth century, reflecting the changes brought about by the Oxford Movement.

Could there have been 'West Gallery singers' at Radley? The churchwardens' records refer to the appointment of a 'singing master' in 1808 (Mr West) and again in 1811 (Mr Cowdry), with payments recorded up to 1812-13. It is likely that it was the Revd John Radcliffe (incumbent from 1807 to 1852) who engaged the singing masters; the figures quoted in Chapter 6 indicate that these singing masters were quite well paid. We also know that the Revd John Radcliffe had a thriving Sunday school, which included children of dissenters, and might therefore have been sympathetic to non-conformists. In addition, there is evidence that he disapproved of the plans by William Sewell and Robert Singleton to set up St Peter's College (now Radley College) in 1847 because of their 'Papist' leanings and their commitment to the Oxford Movement. And, from the opposite point of view, Singleton records in a diary entry for 1847, quoted in Chapter 5, his disapproval of the 'scandalous singing' he encountered on a visit to the Church. No two styles could be more contrasting: the solemnity and purity of music made by trained choristers of the Oxford Movement against the rough and ready enthusiasm of village musicians.

If indeed West Gallery music flourished in Radley, what became of its west gallery? In a letter dated 1868 found in Radley College's archives, the then patron, Sir George Bowyer

(1810-1883) refers to pulling down a gallery 'more than 20 years ago' which one of his ancestors had built for a 'preacher – a Wesleyan' appointed to the post. From his tone and the fact we know he had converted to Roman Catholicism, he obviously disagreed with what was going on: the term 'Wesleyan' suggests a severe disdain for the type of music and the conduct of the congregation at Radley, as well as the attitude of the incumbent. As a final comment, Sir George recounts in the letter that this gallery was pulled down 'against the wishes of the Churchwardens and without asking permission of the Bishop'.

So, the 1801 gallery was removed in the middle of the nineteenth century – to be replaced for other reasons by the existing gallery in 1963. This gallery, with its plain, simple pews, is still used regularly to seat the congregation at services when the chairs and pews below are full.

The 1963 west gallery
Note the photograph was taken before the 2008 reordering.

The tower

Under the gallery at the west end of the Church is access to the bottom of the bell tower. The tower was added to the Church in the fifteenth century, opening up the possibility of hanging large bells. In medieval times, church bells were rung not just for services and celebrations but also for events such as fires and floods.

The tower screen, which divides the tower from the nave, dates from between 1927 and 1929. The original west door has been obscured by a cupboard, as the south door and porch are now the way into the Church.

The bell ringers' gallery in the tower was put in during the 1930s, which meant that the ropes could be shortened. Previously the bells had been rung at ground level and had a reputation for being difficult to handle. It is not known how the ringers reached their new gallery – probably via a ladder or possibly a wooden 'open' staircase.

The bells

Radley Church has six bells, five of which date from 1754 and the other from 1952.

In 1552 a national inventory of church possessions refers to Radley Church having *iij* [three] bells. These are likely to have been large bells similar to the current ones. It is not known how long they had already been there. Sometime between 1552 and 1754 they appear to have been joined by two further large bells, as the churchwardens' accounts record that they decided in 1753 to replace five bells. The churchwardens' reports for 1754 then show that five large bells were replaced at a cost of £51 4s ½d. These were cast by Abel Rudhall of Gloucester, most likely using the metal of the old bells. Rudhalls was a family business of bell founders and, between 1684 and 1835, they are known to have produced over 5,000 bells. Abel Rudhall came to be described as the greatest bell-founder of his age – five bells cast by him still hang in Wells Cathedral.

Radley Church's sanctus bell was cast in 1617 by Henry Knight of Reading. This also is likely to have replaced an earlier one. The sanctus is a smaller bell rung individually as part of the liturgy, not as part of a peal. It is sometimes referred to as a ting-tang and still hangs today in the tower below the other larger bells.

The five large bells were rehung with new woodwork and clappers by Alfred White of Appleton in 1855 to 1856, at a cost of £22 according to the churchwardens' reports.

Another bell, a treble known as the Angelus, was recast by the Mears & Stainbank bell foundry in Whitechapel in 1952 to celebrate the accession of Queen Elizabeth II. The metal was from an earlier bell of 1898 cast by the same foundry to commemorate the Diamond Jubilee of Queen Victoria in 1897. Unfortunately the foundry had not had an opportunity in 1898 to tune this new bell to match those already there and so it had not been a success.

In 1952 all the bells were rehung in a new oak frame made from a Radley oak by Richard White of Appleton (the great-grandson of Alfred White who rehung the bells in 1855 to 1856). The cost of about £400 was raised by a fundraising appeal. A reopening ceremony was carried out on 21 October 1952 with the ringing of peals and prayers of dedication. The bells were hallowed with new names but, except for the Angelus, retained their original inscriptions (see table).

Most recently, in 2014 after a regular survey, Whites of Appleton recommended that urgent work on the gudgeons[2] was necessary. This work would mean dismantling and removing the bells, working on them and then rehanging them with mostly new fittings in the existing frames. The total cost would be in the order of £37,000. Over the weekend of 20-21 June 2015, all the money was raised. Many people connected with the village and Church gave

---

[2] The headstock, which attaches the bell to the wheel, is pivoted on two gudgeons. These strong pins transfer the weight of the bell into the bearings.

generously so that the centuries-old sound of bells ringing out across the village from the Church tower would continue. This continued a long tradition of giving to keep the bells in good order: almost five hundred years ago, Richard Sheen, a Radley husbandman, wrote in his will dated 1558: 'I give and bequeath towards the maintenance of the bell 2 bushels of barley'.

Details of the bells at St James the Great, Radley[1]

Bell	Name (given in 1952)	Inscription	Weight (cwt-qr-lb)	Note
First (the Angelus or treble)	GABRIEL for the Angel Gabriel	Front MEARS & STAINBANK LONDON CAST AND RECAST ME A.M.D.G. ANNO FELICI FIO CAMPANULA VICI MULTAS FELICES PERSONITURA VICES A.S. MDCCCXCVII V.R. LX QUEEN VICTORIA 1898 Back 19(M)52 LET US SING / UNTO THE LORD A NEW SONG QUEEN ELIZABETH II 1952 J.V.PIXELL VICAR A.CROSS & H.GREENING CHURCHWARDENS	3-2-16	G#
Second	MARY for the Virgin Mary	HARK TO OUR MELODY AR 1754	4-0-21	F#
Third	JAMES after James, the patron saint of Radley Church	WHEN YOU US RING WE'LL SWEETLY SING AR 1754	4-1-02	E
Fourth	EDMUND after St Edmund of Abingdon	PEACE AND GOOD NEIGHBOURHOOD AR 1754	4-0-27	D#
Fifth	CHARLES after Bishop Charles Gore, vicar of Radley 1893-1894	PROSPERITY TO THIS PARISH AR 1754	4-2-14	C#
Sixth (tenor)	GEORGE after Sir George Bowyer, patron and benefactor	ABEL RUDHALL OF GLOUCESTER CAST US 1754	5-2-27	B
Sanctus		HENRY KNIGHT MADE ME X6X7	¾ cwt	

[1] Weights, apart from that for the sanctus bell which is estimated, provided by Whites of Appleton, December 2015

The bells were removed on 7/8 September 2015. They were returned to the Church on 10 December and rehung in the tower ready for the Carol Service and Christmas. On

Christmas Day 2015 the bells, newly tuned (in the key of B!) rang out joyously over the parish of Radley to celebrate the birth of Christ as they have done for over 250 years.

Treble being removed, September 2015

Refurbished bells on display in the Church prior to rehanging

Church plate

The unseen contents of the Church interior include the plate found in every Church of England church. The word 'plate' is the collective term for the dishes, bowls, cups and other objects made of gold, silver, pewter or brass which are used to celebrate Holy Communion. Every church is required to provide: a chalice (a goblet or footed cup) for the wine; a paten (a small plate), a ciborium (a covered container) or another vessel for the bread; a basin or plate for the reception of alms; and a flagon or other vessel for bringing the wine to the communion table.

Radley Church possesses a modest collection of plate, though it includes some interesting pieces. The oldest items are a small silver paten, thought to be 'pre-Reformation' and dated 1506-7 (London) but with '1571' in the centre of its upper surface within a rudely cut circle, and a silver chalice hallmarked in London in 1605-6. A silver alms dish dated *c.*1678 (London) bears the arms of Lovelace of Hurley (near Maidenhead). Lady Margaret Stonhouse (died 1695) was a daughter of Richard, 1st Baron Lovelace of Hurley, and the wife of Sir George Stonhouse (died 1675). Lady Margaret's memorial is on the north side of the altar. An impressive silver flagon dated 1705 and bearing the arms of the Stonhouse family was made by the London silversmith, Joseph Ward. The origins of an ornate silver chalice dated 1861 and silver paten dated 1862 by the Victorian ecclesiastical silversmith, John Keith, of London, are unknown.

Some of the items of plate at Radley Church

Alms dish *c.*1768   Flagon 1705   Chalice 1861

Sources

Radley History Club publications

Faith and Heraldry: The Stained Glass in the Church of St James the Great, Radley, Patrick Drysdale, 2011

Radley Farms and Families, 1600-2011, Christine Wootton, 2011

Radley Church and Parish: A Brief History, Radley History Club, 2009

The History of Radley, Patrick Drysdale, Rita Ford, Patricia Groser, Marian Orchard, Ann Parkes and Kay Williams, 2002

Other books

Discovering Church Architecture, Mark Child, 1976

Discovering Churches and Churchyards, Mark Child, 2007

England's Thousand Best Churches, Simon Jenkins, 1999

History of Berkshire, Vol. 4, Victoria County History (VCH), 1924, pp. 410-416

Radley. Ancient Barrows to Modern Parish, Patrick Drysdale, 1985

Radley Church and Parish, Sidney E. Allso, 1971

Radley Women's Institute 1925-2010. Extracts from the minute books compiled by Christine Wootton, 2010

The Church Plate of Berkshire, John W. Walker and Margaret I. Walker, 1927

The Diary of a Country Parson 1758-1802, James Woodforde, ed. John Beresford, 1935

The 1880 Restoration of St Nicolas' Church, Abingdon, R.C.M. Barnes, revised 2000

Archives

Churchwardens' Accounts, Berkshire Record Office

Letter from Sir George Bowyer 1868, Radley College Archives

Monumental inscriptions on memorials in Radley Church and on gravestones in the churchyards, 2000, Radley History Club Archives

Radley Church bells: Material displayed in the Church in June 2015 as part of the fundraising event, Richard Dudding

Research into Lenthall's Canopy in Radley Church, Rosemary Smith, 1990/91, Radley History Club Archives

Radley History Club transcripts of will documents

Websites

Anglicans Online, The Warham Guild, http://anglicansonline.org/special/warham.html

Church of England, Things pertaining to churches, www.churchofengland.org/about-us/structure/churchlawlegis/canons/section-f.aspx

Historic England, List entry for Church of St James, www.historicengland.org.uk/listing/the-list/list-entry/1048324

Oxford Diocesan Guild of Church Bell Ringers, http://odg.org.uk

The Anglican Domain, Church history, http://anglican.org/church/ChurchHistory.html

The Corpus of Romanesque Sculpture in Britain & Ireland, St James the Great, Radley, Berkshire, www.crsbi.ac.uk/site/1348/

West Gallery Music Association, www.wgma.org.uk

Victoria County History, Berkshire, www.british-history.ac.uk/vch/berks

Photographs courtesy of Les Hemsworth, John Huddleston, Joyce Huddleston, Pam McKellen and Daphne Pollard

Chapter 4: The Churchyard and Cemeteries

By Rita and Brian Ford

Beneath those rugged elms, that yew-tree's shade,
Where heaves the turf in many a mould'ring heap,
Each in his narrow cell for ever laid,
The rude forefathers of the hamlet sleep.

Elegy Written in a Country Churchyard by Thomas Gray, 1716-1771

In Radley village we have a Neolithic barrow site which dates back some 4,000 years. We also have a Neolithic and Bronze Age cemetery at the Barrow Hills site (the name 'Barrow Hilles' is probably of Saxon derivation), which is situated on or under The Chestnuts development off Radley Road, Abingdon. It is very likely that we also have an Anglo-Saxon burial site somewhere in the parish. Could this possibly have been on the site of the present parish church? Anglo-Saxon cemeteries are quite well documented in this area and it is thought that quite possibly there was an early church here on this site. The current Church building dates from around 1300 AD (see Chapter 2).

The Abingdon Abbey Monks' Map, thought to date from the mid sixteenth century, shows Radley Church as being surrounded by buildings. Today it is surrounded by its churchyard and is situated at the junction of Church Road and Kennington Road, bounded on the north side by the Vicarage and by the village school in the east. There are two modern cemeteries further down Church Road.

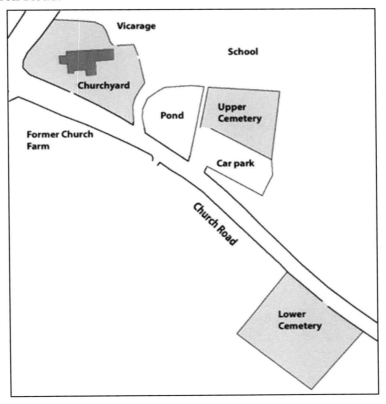

Location of the churchyard and the two cemeteries

About the churchyard

The trees and flowers in the churchyard

Yew trees (*Taxus baccata*), some reputed to be up to a thousand years old and a feature of so many old churchyards, perhaps do have, in some places, pre-Christian associations. However, many were deemed to have first been planted in the time of Edward I (1272-1307), who decreed they should be put outside the front door of a church to protect the building from evil.

Radley Church, 1964
Yew trees can be seen in front of the Church.

The oldest yew tree in Radley's churchyard seems to be the one on the northern boundary and appears to be about 400 years old. The large yew tree in the front of the Church was probably planted in the mid nineteenth century. A photograph in the archives at the Oxfordshire History Centre taken in the early twentieth century at the time of demolition of the blacksmith's smithy, which stood in front of the Church, shows this tree as a young sapling. The other yew trees are fairly modern and have been cut into various shapes.

There can also still be seen 10 lime trees (*Tilia cordata*), some of which are in the churchyard and the remainder on the other side of Kennington Road. These trees are part of a full avenue of lime trees that stretched from Radley Park, where the manor house was situated, to the west door of the Church. This door was the main entrance until the porch was added in the nineteenth century. Obviously at some point a portion of this line of trees was removed when the road was widened.

Churchyards can be a scene of natural beauty in that wild flowers often abound there. At Radley we have flowers such as snowdrops, followed by celandines and primroses, which carpet much of the ground with a profusion of yellow and lemon flowers in spring. It is also a natural haven for all wildlife and birds. Although this does not apply to Radley, it is worth noting that many of the great nineteenth century municipal cemeteries were designed and laid out by the same people who created the public parks. These cemeteries were considered to be places for the public to walk in and enjoy the peace and tranquillity found there.

West end of Radley Church, *c.*1900
The gate and path to the west door are shown together with part of the avenue of lime trees.

The churchyard extension and demolition of the smithy

Although the churchyard now completely surrounds the Church, this was not always so. It was not until Miss Mary Bowyer gave land occupied by the smithy and its surroundings to the vicar and churchwardens in 1897 that the churchyard was able to be extended to its present boundary.

In the January 1898 issue of the parish magazine, the editor wrote:

> The blacksmith suffers by loss of his forge, but the vicar is putting him up in a temporary shed till a new forge is built. The old forge was, perhaps, in olden time some kind of church room. It is not, of course, consecrated but might serve some purpose as a 'church room' again.

The smithy, however, was pulled down. It had stood on land to the south-east corner of the Church. As in Radley, a blacksmith's workplace was usually situated on a main road where easy access could be made for the farmers to bring their horses to be shod and carts to be mended, alongside which there would have been a pond for the smith or farrier to use.

The new piece of land was consecrated for burials on 13 December 1897. According to the parish magazine at that time, it was 'a terribly rough and wet day but all went well with the Bishop of Reading, giving the address'. Records show that the first burials on this final section took place about 1900. New regulations regarding burials came into place about this time which stated that graves had to be put in rows, each separated by a certain distance and at a certain depth.

Impression by an unknown artist of the smithy in front of the Church

In 1988, when the stone walling on the boundary of the school path and the churchyard was being restored by a group including Helen and David Beckett, Joy Alexander and community service boys, a quantity of old nails, horseshoes, hinges and metal objects were found. These are presumed to have come from the old smithy and thought to have been placed behind the stone wall when it was first erected after the demolition of the smithy.

When looking at the churchyard, stone walls can now be seen on most of the boundaries and on further examination it can be seen that very large square and sometimes differently shaped stones have been incorporated into these walls. The question might be asked whether these came originally from the Church. It is possible that a very large square stone in the front wall bounding Church Road could have been a mounting block re-used from the time of the smithy, as early photographs show only a picket fence in this position when the smithy was in use.

The *Church Monthly* magazine for August 1895 records that:

> The churchyard fence had got very unsteady and decayed in parts and repair was necessary. Then, just at the time there was good and seasoned wood out of the old College Chapel for sale much cheaper than we should get it otherwise. It seemed right, therefore, to take the opportunity and get the much needed work done now.

Evidence from old photographs is inconclusive on whether there was a gate on the Church Road side at this time.

Looking after the churchyard

In earlier times it was the church sexton who looked after the churchyard, cutting the grass, digging graves, etc. The *Church Monthly* magazine of 1895 put out an appeal for help to trim the churchyard, and the farmers agreed to send a man each to work on this: 'the trees were shorn, the grass mown and the shrubs cropped', but it needed another day's work to finish the job. At the same time the fence situated on Church Road was thoroughly renewed and painted and the bricks re-set.

In 1937 it was also reported in the magazine that a Mr Grimes had lately retired from the post of sexton after some 50 years. During the 1940s to 1950s, a Mr Turner of Church Road served as the church sexton and part of his work was to light and maintain the solid fuel boiler. An article in the *Radley Parish Magazine* of May 1947 tells us that the sexton and cleaner received £21 9s 6d per year.

The churchyard continues to be looked after and maintained by a volunteer, but two cemeteries are now maintained by contractors. The grave interments are part of the funeral directors' remit.

Nowadays burials and the interment of ashes are allowed only in the Upper Cemetery – the newer of the two cemeteries.

Churchyard layout

In Radley churchyard, as with most other old churchyards, very early graves were marked only with a wooden cross. These of course, over time, have rotted away and so have been lost. It was only when the more prosperous families could afford to have a stone or marble headstone that these have lasted and can now be traced and dated from the inscriptions on them. Consequently it has not been possible for us to mention every grave or interment.

The churchyard can be divided into four sections: north, south, east and west. These are shown in the plan on the next page, which also indicates the area given to the Church by Miss Bowyer in 1897 and the site of the former smithy within this piece of land. The Church Room, built in the early 1980s, is adjacent to the churchyard. A gate near the north-east corner of the churchyard opens into the front garden of the Vicarage. Another gate leads to the Church Room and through to the drive past the School House to the primary school (see Chapter 2).

Below, we take you on a tour of the different sections of the churchyard in turn, concentrating on the most interesting and important graves. This tour is followed by details of key burials in the Lower Cemetery and then a brief description of the Upper Cemetery.

Our village burial records date from 1599 and, as can be seen in this chapter, much information can be gathered from them. An old, numbered map of the churchyard burial ground discovered among the church records, and available on microfiche, records the various graves but no document matching the numbers to names has been found. Today the vicar's secretary (see Chapter 7) adds details of new interments to the appropriate plan on her computer.

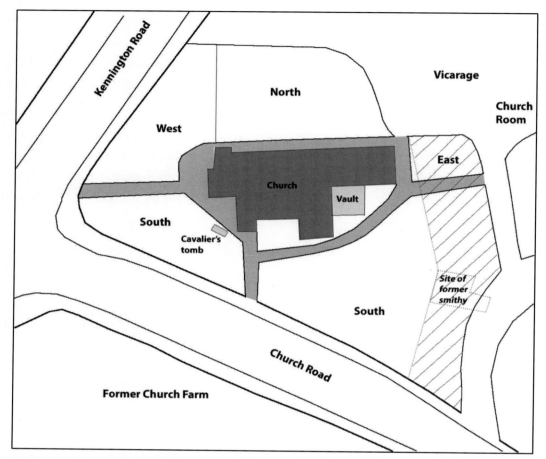

Plan of Radley Church and the sections of its churchyard
The cross-hatched area indicates the extension created from the land given to the Church by Miss Mary Bowyer in 1897. 'Vault' indicates the location of the Stonhouse/Bowyer vault (see South side of the Church).

North side of the Church

Most of the graves we can see today in this area are from the nineteenth century. Based on the burial records and a map of the churchyard, it is estimated that there are about 1,200 graves in this section dating from 1600 to 1936. However, to have had that many interments in this relatively small space over that period of time means that family graves were reused several times and further interments were put on top of others. This was a common practice during earlier years.

The Greenaway family

On this side of the Church we find a rather grand chest tomb for members of the Greenaway family. They were farmers who lived and farmed in the late eighteenth century at what is now known as Lower Farm. The railings have been removed from this tomb – probably requisitioned during the Second World War to gather as much metal as possible for the war effort.

The Hutchins family

Gravestones dating from the late eighteenth to the early nineteenth century to the memory of members of the Hutchins family can also be found in this area. Edmund Hutchins was farming 262 acres at Neat Home Farm, Lower Radley, in 1768 according to a farm tenancies survey. His descendants were still there in the early nineteenth century. Edmund and his wife, Mary, had at least eight children who were baptised in Radley Church.

Gravestones of the Hutchins family

The Badcock family (see also West side)

Members of this family who died in the early to mid-eighteenth century are buried here. They lived and farmed at Wick Hall. Graves noted by Oxfordshire Family History Society's records show that in this section there are the graves of:

John and Joseph Badcock, sons of Richard and Lois Badcock, who died in infancy.

Mary Badcock, wife of Joses, who died in 1861. Also Susannah their daughter who died in 1851 aged 17.

Eliza Badcock, daughter of Joses and Mary, who died in 1812 in the 'sixth year of her age'.

Joses Badcock who died aged 47 in 1818.

Henry Badcock, son of John and Thirza, who was born and died in 1838. Also their daughter Sarah Bennett who died in 1840 aged 6.

Eliza Badcock, daughter of Richard and Mary Badcock, who died in 1809 aged 34.

Benjamin Badcock, son of Richard and Lois, who died in 1811 aged 24.

Lois Badcock who died in 1811 aged 55. Richard her husband who died in 1814 aged 71 is also buried here.

Sarah Badcock, daughter of Richard and Mary, who died in 1803 aged 29.

Richard Eason

Richard Eason was the village blacksmith who worked in the smithy situated alongside the Church (see above) and who died in 1806. His headstone is carved with two daisy rings, which were the symbols used on stables and barns to keep evil spirits at bay. This headstone appears to be inscribed on the reverse side as do all the other headstones in this row. It is not known why this was done.

Detail of carved headstone for Richard Eason

George Silvester

Another blacksmith who worked at the smithy was George Silvester who died in 1881 and is buried here, as is his wife, Harriet, who died in 1902. George lived in a cottage opposite the Church and combined his work at the smithy with keeping the village post office.

William Shire?

On an old plan of Radley churchyard, 'A very old tomb' is marked on the north-east boundary corner nearest to the Vicarage. But it has not been possible to ascertain just how old it is and whose it is. However, the first entry in the Radley burial records says: 'Here lyeth the body of William Shire. He deceased the 28.... his age was 33 yeares'. This entry was made before 1599. Might this have been his grave?

Mary Queen

The Radley burial register dated December 1809 shows that an infant daughter aged 6 months of Mary Queen was buried here. Mary was listed as a vagrant. Child mortality in these early years was very high regardless of whether they came from the highest born families or the lowest. Very many small headstones can be seen throughout the churchyard, mostly around the perimeter where small spaces were available. Unfortunately the inscriptions on many of them have been lost.

Richard Ellis

A long oblong stone monument marks the grave of Richard Ellis. A widower, he had married a widow, Sophia Wells, in 1854. Sophia was born in Radley in about 1802, the daughter of Joses and Mary Badcock. Richard's gravestone states that he was the 'Late Manager of Abingdon Union Workhouse', which was situated in Oxford Road, Abingdon. Richard died on 22 October 1863, aged 73 years at his home in East St Helen's Street in Abingdon. Richard was also clerk to the Guardians of the Poor of the Abingdon Union and frequently posted advertisements in *Jackson's Oxford Journal*, one of which is reproduced below.

TO SURGEONS

The Guardians of the Poor of the Abingdon Union, in the county of Berks, will be ready at their meeting on Thursday the 30th inst. to receive application from fully qualified Medical Practitioners willing to undertake the duties of Medical Officer for the Second District of the said Union; comprising one-half of the Borough of St Helen, Abingdon, and the parish of Radley and Sunningwell, all adjoining the aforesaid parish of St Helen, the salary of which will be £80 per annum, exclusive of 1s. 6d per case of vaccination, 15s for each case of midwifery, and the fees allowed by the Poor Law Board for all cases of accident; and the duties of the said District to commence on Thursday the 6th of September next.

By order of the Board
Richard Ellis (Clerk)
Board Room, Abingdon, August 9, 1849

In 1835, soon after Richard was appointed as the governor of Abingdon workhouse, an attempt was made on his life. A shot was fired from the workhouse garden into the governor's sitting room, just missing Richard and his sister; it is thought to have been by someone protesting at the introduction of the new regime.

East side of the Church

East side of the churchyard at Radley Church
The shaped yew trees can be seen in the background.

The section on the east side of the Church was incorporated into the churchyard when Mary Bowyer donated land, including the smithy site, towards the end of the nineteenth century (see above). An old photograph held at the Oxfordshire History Centre shows this piece of land, which was to the rear of the smithy, previously being cultivated with vegetables as it was at that time attached to the School House (see Chapter 2).

At the east end of the churchyard we have the graves of some of the more prosperous and wealthy parishioners and here can be seen the most elaborate of the monuments.

Sir George Henry Bowyer

Sir George Henry Bowyer, the last Baronet of Radley, is buried here. He died on 27 September 1950 aged 80 at a nursing home in Falmouth. His father is buried on the south side of the Church, though not in the family vault also on the south side (see below).

Revd Charles Boxall Longland

The gravestone is inscribed:

> In loving memory of Charles Boxall Longland vicar of Radley 1896-1916 and Rector of Aston Tirrold 1917-1937. Called to rest 8 Dec 1940 in his 79th year.

> In loving memory of Gertrude Martha (Longland) the beloved wife of the Revd C.B. Longland vicar of this parish who fell asleep in Jesus 3rd April 1905.

More details of the Revd Longland are given in Chapter 5.

Harold Edward Betteridge

Nearby is a monument to Harold Edward Betteridge, Royal Marine Artillery, No. 16660. Betteridge enlisted in the First World War when he was aged 17 years, 11 months and 30 days and was found to be one day under age. He was posted to 'Q' Company, Royal Marine Artillery training base at Eastney, Hampshire. Unfortunately he became ill and died of pneumonia on 27 September 1918, just a few weeks after joining up. He is also remembered on both war memorials inside the Church where a brass plaque on the north wall commemorates those who died in the two world wars and a wooden tablet at the back of the Church lists the 64 Radley men who served in the First World War.

Harold was the nephew of Francis Frederick Betteridge who farmed at Lower Farm. His mother had died soon after he was born, so he was brought up in Radley at the home of his uncle. Francis Betteridge's only son, who died in 1895, is buried in the south-west area of the churchyard.

Josephine Dockar-Drysdale

Mrs Dockar-Drysdale of Wick Hall, Radley, who died on 14 March 1921, is buried here along with her grandson, Andrew John Watkins Drummond Dockar-Drysdale, who died on 7 April 1910 when only a few days old. He was the infant son of William and Ellen Eirene

Watkiss Dockar-Drysdale, who are buried along with several of their later children and other members of the Dockar-Drysdale family in the Lower Cemetery (see below).

Ann Agnes Mace

Almost all of the monuments in this section consist of a marble cross on a three-tiered stepped base except that of Ann Agnes Mace, who died in April 1908 aged 73 years. Her headstone is of a beautiful pink marble and sculpted into a large scroll. The parish records show that she was a visitor at Wick Hall, Radley, but died at the Acland Nursing Home, Oxford. Ann's husband, Stephen George Mace, who had been a librarian in London, died in April 1920 at the age of about 84, and was buried in the same grave.

**The Dockar-Drysdale tomb in the foreground
with the marble scroll tomb of Ann Agnes Mace at the rear**

Revd John Vincent Pixell

John Vincent Pixell was the vicar of Radley from 1941 to 1959. His ashes were buried here in September 1965. More details about him can be found in Chapter 5.

George Kenneth Silvester

George Kenneth Silvester died on 15 December 1930 at the age of 44 in Oxford's isolation hospital. It is worth noting that George's grave is orientated north–south and not east–west as all of the others are. Was this because there was a shortage of room in this section? His wife Rose, who died in 1956, is buried alongside him. George was the grandson of George Silvester, who is buried in the north side of the Church (see above), and the son of Jethro and Harriet Silvester, who are buried in the south side (see below).

Adam Fettiplace Blandy and Elizabeth Blandy

An interesting grave here is that of Adam and Elizabeth Blandy. Adam Blandy had built and lived at The Warren, a large house on Radley Road, Abingdon. This house later became the Warren Hospital. It was pulled down in the 1980s and a housing estate called 'The Warren' was built on the site. Their son Captain Robert Blandy, of the Colonial Defence Force, served in the Boer War and was killed in 1901 in action at Molteno, South Africa, and is buried there. His grave, which is some 6,000 miles away from Radley, is almost identical to that of his parents who are resting here.

Adam, a civil engineer, was born in Longworth. He married Anne Elizabeth Mary Nicholl and they had 13 children. Their eldest, Blanche Gwendolyn, married James Lees Norton, a solicitor, and his grave is nearby. The Nortons lived at Braeside, Whites Lane, Radley.

**The grave of James Lees Norton who died in 1922 and his elder daughter
Josephine Elizabeth Margaret Mason who died in 2000 aged about 96**

South side of the Church

South of the path from the Church Room to the Church, in the section where the smithy used to be, the earliest burials marked here start just after 1900. Growing here is a rowan tree (mountain ash) which was presented and planted by Radley Women's Institute to commemorate their 70th anniversary in October 1995. In recent years, interments of ashes have taken place near the beech hedge on the Church Road side.

Most of the headstones at the south facing front of the Church are dated in the eighteenth century. Unfortunately, probably due to the early date of these and acid rain, most inscriptions are now lost but here again we find that the inscription appears to have been on the reverse side of the headstone.

Martha Ann Foster

In December 1936 the burial took place of Martha Foster, née Weston. She was the village's midwife. Her grave is situated by the junction of the school path and the path leading to the Vicarage. The vicar at the time of her funeral, the Revd Francis Daly Briscoe said it was:

> With the sadness of farewell that we laid to rest in the old Churchyard, one who was of the older residents of Radley. Their places cannot be filled, and their departure makes yet another shadow on the path of life here. May her soul rest in the Peace and Mercy of God.

Martha Ann Weston, who was born in 1860, married John James Foster who worked for the Great Western Railway.

Left: grave of Martha Foster in 1936   **Right: Stonhouse/Bowyer family vault**

Stonhouse/Bowyer vault

If we look towards the south wall of the chancel, we see the family vault of the Stonhouse and Bowyer families (see Chapter 1 and Appendix 2) built *c.*1674. In his will Sir George Stonhouse, who died in 1674/5, stated his wish to be buried in the newly completed vault, which was accessed through a trap door under the choir stalls. The Bowyers continued the tradition, starting with Admiral Sir George Bowyer, 1st Baronet Bowyer of Radley, in 1800. The 3rd Baronet, also George, who died in London in 1883, was the last to be buried in the vault. In 1860 he had arranged for the body of his father, who had died in Dresden, to be brought back to be interred in the family vault. *Jackson's Oxford Journal* of 29 September 1860 reports that:

> … the body was disinterred and arrived from London by the Great Western Railway on Thursday afternoon, in charge of Mr. Cavell, undertaker, of this city, and was deposited the same evening in the family vault.

In his *History of Radley College 1847-1947*, A.K. Boyd tells how Warden Sewell:

> … brought out the torch stands ... and lit Radley churchyard with them when in 1860 old Sir George Bowyer … was buried at dead of night.

Sir William Bowyer, 4th Baronet, who died in 1893, was buried in Brighton where he lived. There is a memorial tablet to him on the south side of the chancel of Radley Church. The graves of his younger brother, Henry George, and his nephew, Sir George Henry, 5th Baronet, are in the south and east side, respectively, of the churchyard at Radley.

Charles Ambridge

In the row next to Martha Foster's grave there is a granite block marking the resting place of Charles Ambridge, 1832-1910. Charles worked at Radley Station for some 20 years as stationmaster. Also buried here is his wife Hannah, who died on 17 December 1916.

Thomas West

To the right side of the porch is a very imposing tomb (vault). This is for Thomas West who died in 1857 aged 80. He was a surgeon, apothecary and midwife, and an early pioneer in the discovery of diseases. He wrote a paper in 1813-14 on his observations of puerperal (childbirth) fever and its connection with erysipelas in the Abingdon area. Many years later it was discovered that both diseases were caused by streptococcus; in the days of poor hygiene, it was being carried on the hands of the surgeon or midwife from one patient to another.

The tomb of Thomas West near the porch

The inscription on his tomb reads:

> In memory of Thomas West Esq. of the Manor House, Sutton Courtenay, Berks, who died January 22nd 1857 aged 80.

If we look at the West tomb, the roof of an earlier vault can be clearly seen at ground level. This suggests that Thomas West's parents and younger brother William were buried here before the later addition was added above ground for Thomas West.

This tomb has had its iron railings removed as with other monuments in the churchyard.

The Cavalier's tomb

Approximately 2.5 metres south-west of the Church porch is a chest tomb known as the Cavalier's tomb. It is likely to have been for a Cavalier soldier who died during the Civil War. According to parish records, there were two gentlemen whose tomb it could possibly have been: Capt. Thomas Gylburke under 'Eellswell Lansford's regiment' [probably Sir Thomas Lunsford of the King's Army] and Capt. Ltn. Umphrey Baines 'under Colonel Bellosis' [probably Colonel John Bellasis]. However, no inscription can be seen on this tomb and so we can only surmise that one or maybe even both of these officers is buried here.

Gylburke and Baines both died in 1643, a year when burial records show an extremely high mortality rate for the village (see Chapter 2). Many of those buried were born in Radley. The cause of death for most of these people would have been typhus or influenza, although it was often known as morbus campestris (camp fever). The overcrowded, unhygienic conditions in Oxford due to the Civil War caused this fever to spread rapidly among the population of Oxford and surrounding villages.

The tomb is Grade II listed. Its listing on the Historic England website describes it as:

> C17. Limestone. Central recessed moulded panel with worn cherub's head flanked by 2 panels of relief-carved Tudor roses set within recessed roundels: similar roundels to sides and rear.

The Cavalier's tomb

Henry George Bowyer

In the south-west corner of this section is a flat memorial stone in memory of Henry George Bowyer, who died at Leamington Spa on 26 September 1883 aged 70. He was the son of Sir George Bowyer (1783-1860) and Lady Ann Hammond Bowyer. When his older brother, Sir William, died without issue in 1893, the title of 5th Baronet of Radley and 9th Baronet of Denham went to Henry George's son, George Henry, who is buried in the east side of the churchyard (see above).

Thomas Alexander Voss

Also here we find another large flat stone monument. This one is to Thomas Alexander Voss, who was born in 1810 at Chimsurah, in Bengal, India, and died on 3 October 1833 at Radley Hall during the period when Benjamin Kent was renting Radley Hall (see Chapter 1).

The Stone family

One of the tombs is to Joseph Powell Stone, son of Charles and Jane Stone, who died 21 September 1858 aged 10 years. Another is to Jane Stone who died on 24 January 1881 aged 64 years. Included on the stone are inscriptions which read:

> Sacred to the memory of Fanny Jane, daughter of Charles and Jane Stone who died March 6th 1871 aged 13 years

> Sacred to the memory of Charles Stone who died May 12th 1860 aged 60 years

The Stone family farmed at Neat Home Farm.

The Stone family grave   **The Gould family grave**

The Gould family

Nearby is the grave of the Gould family. James Gould was a gardener for the Bowyer family in 1811 and lived in a cottage in Radley Park. He was a steward to Sir George Bowyer (1783-1860) and eventually became a farmer. When the Great Western Railway wanted to build a track through Sir George's land in 1837, James represented him and opposed its building. The founder of Radley College, Robert Corbet Singleton, had problems with Gould at times. Eventually after losing his family, James retired to Spring Road, Abingdon, and became a tea dealer. Names on his tomb are as follows.

> Henry Gould who died on September 27th in the 31st year of his life
>
> James Gould died 19th February 1853 aged 67
>
> Frederick Robert Gould, his son born 13th April 1813, died 14th Jun 1858
>
> Jemima Cecily Bennett, daughter of James E.M. Gould and wife of Alfred Bennett, born 28 September 1809 and died 28 September 1841
>
> Sacred to the memory of Elfrida Matilda Gould, the wife of James who departed this life July 7th 1822 aged 30 years

Elfrida had given birth to her youngest child, Matilda Sarah Dorothy on 29 June 1822, so her death most likely had a connection with that event.

The Coleing family

This section has several headstones for the Coleing family who were farmers at Sugworth Farm. The family originated in Binfield, but were in Radley in 1737 when Thomas Coleing was baptised in the Church. The family farmed at Sugworth Farm for many years until John Coleing left in about 1873.

Gravestones of George Coleing (d. 1825) and his wife Mary

Gravestones of William Coleing (d. 1828) and his wife Mary

It is thought these headstones have been relocated at some time from another part of the cemetery.

West side of the Church

John Oldrey Hingston

Near the west door is an ornamental headstone to John Oldrey Hingston, who was the foreman of works and died during the building of St Peter's Chapel, Radley College, in 1895. John was baptised on 20 June 1838 at Blackawton, Devon, the son of Richard Hingston and Grace Collins (née Oldrey). He married Elizabeth Durham and they had 10 children.

The Davis family

The Davis family have a very ornate headstone and grave, which is bounded by short iron railings. It records the death of the following members of the family.

> In remembrance of Morris who died February 11th 1848 aged 4 months and of Charles who died September 21st 1861 aged 6 years and 6 months children of James Morris and Elizabeth Davis
>
> Also of James Morris Davis who died October 23rd 1869 aged 47 years
>
> Also Elizabeth his widow who died October 6th 1914 aged 87 years

Davis family plot

Edwin George and Jane Monk

Edwin George Monk, a doctor of music, was the first precentor at Radley College. His grave is marked with a cross on a pedestal. *Jackson's Oxford Journal* of Saturday 6 January 1900 gives a full account of his funeral. The service was conducted by the Revd C.B. Longland and Revd Basil-Cole, and accompanied by the choir. The procession then passed out to the grave, close to the tower, and the deceased was buried in a polished oak coffin on which was inscribed 'EDWIN GEORGE MONK, Died January 3rd, 1900, aged 80 years'. The newspaper article also lists the many relatives and friends who were present at the funeral.

In 1859 Monk was appointed the organist at York Minster. After nearly 25 years of service there, he returned to Radley and lived at East Cottage (now 75 Foxborough Road) at the end of St James Road. His wife Jane died in York in 1882 and is buried alongside him. The organ in Radley Church was installed in his memory (see Chapter 3).

The Curtis family

In the north-west corner of the churchyard we find a very ornate flat stone memorial with an embellished cross lying flat on top. This grave, which appears to have had iron railings surrounding it, is that of the Curtis family. Inscriptions are as follows:

> In memory of Charles Archer Curtis of Abingdon born 20th September 1807 died 31st July 1855

> Also of Charles Archer, son of the above and Elizabeth his wife, born 2nd April 1835 died 29th August 1835 and was buried in St Helen's churchyard, Abingdon

> Also of Harriet Curtis, his mother, born 9th February 1775 died 8th February 1860

> And of Adelaide Elizabeth Boys his only grandchild born 2nd June 1858 died 23rd July 1859

Charles Curtis was a solicitor in Abingdon in 1841. He married Elizabeth Butt in Little Hampton, Sussex, in 1828.

Jethro and Harriet Silvester

Jethro died in 1926 and Harriet his wife died in 1933. Jethro was a blacksmith before becoming the licensee of the Bowyer Arms in Radley. On his retirement he built the house called Fairfield, which is across the road from the pub, next to the present village shop. He also was joint owner of Sugworth Farm with his son, George Kenneth Silvester (see above).

Revd George Wharton

Revd George Wharton, who died on 23 December 1925, was a curate at Radley from 1876 to 1883. He was also a fellow and precentor of Radley College. More details about him are given in Chapter 5.

The Badcock family (see also North side)

Further members of the Badcock family, who were tenants at Wick Farm, have a large chest tomb along with several other graves in the north-west section of the churchyard. The inscriptions, recorded during a survey by Oxfordshire Family History Society, read:

> In memory of John Badcock who died October 19th 1867 aged 70 years

> Mary Ellen Badcock died September 14th 1922 aged 86 years

> Elizabeth Mary, wife of George Henry Badcock 1839-1927

> George Henry Badcock born September 28th 1839 died July 23rd 1932

James Lewis Badcock born September 17th 1828 died September 29th 1862

Thirza wife of John Badcock who died July 7 1887 aged 89 years

Sarah Bennett Badcock born June 21 1834 died October 22 1840

Sarah Sophia Badcock born July 11 1841 died January 17 1852

Henry Badcock born March 31st 1838 died November 10 1838

Family vault of John and Thirza Badcock of Wick Farm

Graves nearby are to: Thirza Shrimpton of Shinfield, Berkshire, daughter of John and Thirza Badcock, and who died in 1861 aged 30 years; and to Florence Julia and George Stanley Badcock, who died in 1927 and 1964 respectively. There is also a grave to Bessie Mildred Badcock, born in 1875, and who died in 1923.

The Badcock family tomb

The most recent interment in this section was of remains found in the Church during the renovations following the death watch beetle infestation (see Chapter 2). Archaeologists examined the tombs under the floor of the Church when the floor was removed and bones were found there. It is possible that they were members of the Porter family as they had requested they should be buried inside the Church. Thomas Porter who died in 1544 wrote in his will: 'My body is to be buried within the Chapel of Radley before St John's altar'. A large stone with an inscription to members of the Porter family was found under the lectern in the Church. Christopher Porter, who died in 1572/3, also requested that his body should be buried in the Church as did Thomas Porter of Thrupp in 1612 and John Porter in 1578. Other members of the family requested a burial in the churchyard.

Another will, that of Thomas Palmer of Radley dated 21 July 1599, stated that:

> I bequeath my soul to the pity and mercy of Almighty God and my body to be buried in the Church of Radley in the aisle called Our Ladies Aisle and in consideration I give unto the Church 6s 8d more than ordinary.

The Lower Cemetery

This cemetery, which is situated further down Church Road, was consecrated in about 1930 when the first burials took place. By this time the churchyard was full.

View of the Lower Cemetery from Church Road

In the centre of the cemetery is a weatherworn octagonal stone, believed to be thirteenth century. Research suggests it could be the lower base of the font from Sandford Church as it corresponds in size and antiquity to it. This is presumed to have been in Sandford Church in the 1840s but was taken out of it sometime after that. The next mention of this great stone is reported as being:

> in the grass by the roadside on top of Pebble Hill by Radley Great Wood on the other side of the Thames, used perhaps as a mounting-block for horsemen.

This usage has been confirmed by local people within living memory. It was removed from there to its present position in the cemetery in 1935.

The stone in the centre of the Lower Cemetery

Revd Thomas Digby Raikes

Thomas Raikes was formerly a master at Radley College and was buried in the Lower Cemetery in 1934. His wife Elizabeth, who died in 1948, is also buried here. Their plot is situated near to the central crossing. Their only child, Second Lieutenant John Francis Raikes, was killed in action at the Somme on 10 October 1916.

Thomas was born in India in about 1850 and came to Radley in 1879. He married Elizabeth Higgins in 1885 in the Cheltenham area. While at Radley he and his wife played an active part in the life of the church and community and, when he left in 1895 to become vicar of Marcham, they were greatly missed. By the time of the 1911 Census they had moved to Whichford Rectory, Shipston-on-Stour.

The Povey family

In this cemetery there is also a grave that holds the remains of Albert and Maud Povey, who lived in Church Road. The names of their six children, Phyllis, Phoebe, Fred, Pansy, Pearl and George, who all died at a very early age, have been added to their headstone.

Ronald Arthur Engelbretson Coke and Alfred Thomas Baber

There are two Second World War graves placed in this cemetery by the War Graves Commission. 1443022 Aircraftman 2nd Class R.A.E. Coke died on 12 April 1943 aged 21. He was the son of Arthur Bernard and Ethel Thorne Coke. The other grave belongs to 770790 Sergeant A.T. Baber, who was serving in the RAF, but died in 1941 aged 33 as a result of a motor accident.

The Dockar-Drysdale family

Situated in the far right hand corner of this cemetery is a large family plot for the Dockar-Drysdale family from Wick Hall, where several members of the family have been laid to rest, including Josephine Dockar-Drysdale's only son, William, and his wife, Ellen Eirene.

The Allison family

On the extreme left hand side from the entrance gate there are the graves of the Allison family, who lived in Lower Radley. They include:

Captain George Allison, late King's Company, Grenadier Guards, who died 9 May 1932 aged 62 years and his wife Martha, who died 21 January 1943 aged 72 years

Their third son, Captain Rupert Edward Allison who died 31 October 1988 aged 80 and his wife, Betty, who died 18 June 1986 aged 73 years

Their fourth son, Captain Robert Villiers Allison, who died 7 May 1975 aged 64

Their eldest daughter, Natalie Jane Darroch née Allison, born 1899, died 14 June 1989, Queen's Army schoolmistress

The Upper Cemetery

The Upper Cemetery, next to the village school, is the latest piece of land to be used for burials and the interment of ashes. It was consecrated on 7 October 1996 by the Bishop of Reading, the Rt Revd John Bone. In 2000, to celebrate the Millennium, a time capsule was buried in this burial ground. It can be dug up for examination of its contents in the year 2101.

View from the entrance to the Upper Cemetery

On reflection

Although we no longer have those 'rugged elms' that once shaded our churchyard and cemeteries, here we are some five hundred years later and the forefathers of this parish are still being laid to rest in the same area that their ancestors would have known.

Sources

Discovering Churches and Churchyards, Mark Child, 2007

Early Modern Radley: People, Land and Buildings, 1547-1768, Richard Dudding, 2014

Excavations at Barrow Hills, Radley, Alistair Barclay and Claire Halpin, 1998

Gone for a Soldier, M.B.J. Mawhinney, 2010

Jackson's Oxford Journal

The English Heartland, Robert and Monica Beckinsale, 1980

Radley Farms and Families, 1600 - 2011, Christine Wootton, 2011

Radley History Club transcripts of will documents

Radley, Monumental Inscriptions, 1709 to 1993, Oxfordshire Family History Society

Radley News, September 1988

Radley, Register of Burials (1599-1980), transcribed by Oxfordshire Family History Society

The Boer War Casualty Roll 1899-1902

The Parish Church of St Andrew, Sandford on Thames: A Historical Guide, Liz Shatford, (available from www.sandfordchurch.org.uk/TheChurch.aspx)

Photographs courtesy Brian Ford and Christine Wootton

Chapter 5: Clergy of St James the Great, Radley

by Christine Wootton

This chapter lists, in approximate date order, all the clergy who are known to have been appointed in some role to St James the Great. About some we know very little. Others were significant figures, whether because of their role in the Radley community or because of wider fame (or infamy!).

The changing status of Radley Church and its clergy

To make sense of the entries some prior explanation is needed of the status of Radley Church and its clergy, and who appointed them, which has changed considerably over time. These changes also tell us much about the changing character of the village and who had the dominant influence.

The earliest known document about the Church is a deed dated 15 March 1271 setting out the responsibilities of John de Clifford, vicar of St Helen's Church in Abingdon, who was appointed by Abingdon Abbey. His duties included the provision of 'fit chaplains' for three 'chapels', one of which was Radley. This meant that the vicar of St Helen's was also the vicar of Radley, although Radley also had its own chaplain. The 1271 deed indicates that the chaplain lived at least part of the time in Radley, in the 'house with the croft, where the chaplains serving Radley were wont to abide'. This wording also tells us that these arrangements had been going on for some time before 1271.

Since then there have been major changes. Some have happened gradually, but uncertainty and dispute are recorded in some cases.

The Reformation

The very earliest Radley vicars and chaplains were part of the Roman Catholic Church. In the 1530s, Henry VIII became head of a separate Church of England, severing the link with Rome and gaining access to the enormous wealth of the monasteries. Abingdon Abbey was dissolved in 1538. Since then Radley Church and its incumbents have been part of the established Church of England, other than a brief return to Roman Catholicism in the reign of Queen Mary (1553-1558). The split with Rome probably did not have significant early impact on the substance of religious ceremony and teaching in Radley Church but, by the early seventeenth century, we have evidence of the changes in train. John Herbert, incumbent from about 1622 to 1668, had sufficiently radical Protestant leanings as a young man to have caused his arrest and expulsion from Oxford University.

The dissolution of Abingdon Abbey, the dominant force in the area, also changed local power structures. As well as appointing the vicar of St Helen's, the Abbey had held the Manor of Radley. In 1560 a rising gentry family, the Stonhouses, purchased the Manor (see Chapter 1) and this had a significant effect on the status of Radley Church and its incumbents.

From chapel to church in its own right

In the early sixteenth century there are still references to Radley being a chapel but, by the seventeenth century, Radley has every appearance of being an independent church. For instance, there are separate parish registers for Radley of baptisms, marriages and burials dating from 1599 with incumbents describing themselves therein as 'vicars' rather than 'chaplains', and wills of this time refer to the 'church', 'vicar' and 'vicarage' of Radley. There is no documentary evidence at this time of a formal change having occurred but, in practice, it seems clear that the power of appointment of the incumbent had passed from the vicar of St Helen's to the lord of Radley Manor, who had in effect become patron of an independent living.

The first documentary evidence of a change in status is much later, in May 1783, in the responses given by the vicar of St Helen's to a routine survey by Bishop Barrington of Salisbury. One of the questions related to the chapels in his parish. He replied that he had Radley and Drayton annexed to his living. The parishioners for Drayton usually found their own officiating minister but, for Radley, the Stonhouse family nominated someone. Although the vicar was instituted and inducted to both, he only got the 'trifling acknowledgement sum of 3s 4d from Drayton and 5s from Radley'.

The formal separation of Radley from St Helen's followed some 70 years later. According to *Radley Church and Parish* by Sydney Allso (vicar of Radley from 1966 to 1971):

> In 1836 the archdeaconry of Berkshire was transferred from the diocese of Salisbury to that of Oxford, and by an Order in Council of September 11th 1854, the advowson of St Helen's and St Nicolas', with the chapelries of Drayton and Shippon, passed to the bishop of Oxford, but there was no mention of Radley. … Nathaniel Dodson, who had been vicar of St Helen's since 1824, in order to bring to an end all dispute about Radley had presented the living to Bishop Wilberforce [of Oxford]. … it would seem that the separation of Radley from St Helen's was effected at a date between 1845 and 1854.

In *The Church and Parish of St Nicolas, Abingdon, and other Papers*, Arthur Preston writes:

> Since the Dissolution of the Abbey in 1538 the right of presentation to both St Helen and St Nicolas had been in the hands of the Crown, but in 1854 an exchange of patronage rights between the Crown and the Bishop of Oxford was effected. Under this exchange the advowson of St Nicolas and St Helen's passed to the Bishop. Nothing was said about the chapelries of Radley and Sandford. Radley had for centuries emancipated itself and Sandford at that date was without a church.

The right to appoint the vicar

Although Radley by 1854 was now an independent parish with its own vicar, a dispute remained as to who had the 'advowson' or the legal right to appoint the vicar. As we have seen, appointments had for some time been made in practice by the Stonhouse family. Their successors as lords of the Manor, the Bowyers, strongly asserted this right and did not accept that it had been passed to the Bishop of Oxford. In technical terms they believed the living was a 'donative', entirely in their own gift and independent of the bishop's jurisdiction.[1]

Matters came to a head in 1867 to 1868. Sir George Bowyer (1810-1883) had converted to Roman Catholicism and so could no longer exercise his family's right to appoint. Meanwhile Radley College (see Chapter 1) was anxious to have influence over future appointments because it had encountered hostility from the then incumbent, John Radcliffe, at the time of its founding in 1847. In 1867 Sir George sold to the College the right to make the next appointment and in 1868 the College appointed its warden, William Wood, as vicar. Sir George asked a price of £200 but it is not known if this was the amount paid. There seems to have been some confusion as to whether he was selling just this appointment or the permanent right of appointment (the advowson), but the latter was not the case. We know from Revd Allso's account that he must either have sold three appointments, or initially just one with the next two being sold later.

The Bishop of Oxford, Samuel Wilberforce, refused to accept Radley College's right to appoint, demanding legal proof and asserting it was for him to 'institute' the new vicar. The College did not back down, partly because it believed the living was 'donative' and partly because it wanted to avoid antagonising Sir George Bowyer. Despite not receiving any legal proof, and after a bitter dispute during which Wood was threatened with inhibition (that is, banned from performing his religious duties), the Bishop reluctantly gave way on condition that Wood took 'Oaths' (that is, he swore the oath of allegiance to the Crown and the oath of canonical obedience to the bishop).

The primary antagonists in this dispute were Sir George and the Bishop. The strength of Sir George's views is made clear in a letter dated 23 September 1868, held in Radley College's archives. William Wood was caught in the middle. He felt that Sir George was correct in it being a 'donative' living but he did not want to upset the Bishop.

The appointment of Wood as vicar was the start of a period of some 90 years when Radley College was the dominant influence over Radley's church. Having bought the right to appoint the next two vicars, in 1892 the College purchased the advowson (see Chapter 1). In the following year, Charles Gore was the first vicar to be 'instituted', bringing to an end the dispute with the Bishop.

As described in Chapter 1, the creation of the Benefice of Radley and Sunningwell in 1990 led to a change whereby Radley College and the Diocesan Board of Patronage exercised the right of presentation alternately. In February 2015 the parish of Kennington joined the benefice with the right of presentation to be exercised jointly by the Bishop of Oxford, the Diocesan Board of Patronage and Radley College.

---

[1] It was quite common at the time for the dominant local landowner to have the right of advowson, enabling them to choose the vicar to be appointed, but in most cases they still had to 'present' their choice to the bishop to be formally 'instituted'. Donatives, which were relatively unusual, differed in that the owner of the advowson could make the actual appointment without institution by the bishop.

Vicar or some other status?

The gradual change from the incumbent of Radley being a chaplain to having the status of vicar of Radley has been the subject of much confusion over the years. The parish registers and other contemporary documents such as wills describe the incumbent variously as 'vicar', 'rector' and 'minister'. This seems to have been a matter of imprecise language rather than denoting any real difference between individuals or change over time in the status of the incumbent. At the time of the dispute between Radley College and the Bishop of Oxford over the appointment, there was some suggestion that the status was that of a 'rector' rather than 'vicar'. Old documents and lawyers were consulted in 1894 and it was decided that the incumbent was indeed a 'vicar'.

This chapter is happy to call a 'vicar' a 'vicar'. However, some distinctions in language might help, especially as the list of clergy below covers all those currently known to have served Radley Church in some capacity. Terms in relation to Radley are used in this book as follows:

- **Chaplain**: the incumbent of Radley during the early period (up to about 1600) when Radley was a chapel of St Helen's Church, Abingdon and was not independent in practical terms from St Helens;

- **Vicar**: the incumbent of Radley after it became independent in practical terms from St Helen's Abingdon (from about 1600);

- **Incumbent**: both of the above;

- **Curate**: a person appointed to assist Radley's vicar – increasingly the case from the nineteenth century (curates typically stayed for a very short time, often only a year);

- **Additional clergy**: a person who sometimes officiated in Radley services, but who had no ongoing appointment to the parish;

- **Other titles**: these are used only where there is a distinct status not covered by the above;

- **Clergy**: all of the above.

On occasion the entry for a clergyman quotes directly from a contemporary source that uses different terminology. In such cases, the quotation has not been changed.

Chronological listing of the clergy

The list starts in the mid sixteenth century because this is when we first know who held the incumbency at Radley. For much of the period covered by the list there were vicars and curates serving at the same time and hence some dates overlap. A list of the main incumbents from this time is given in Appendix 3.

Some vicars of St Helen's are included in the list of clergy during the period up to about 1850 when they continued to have legal, even if not practical, responsibilities in Radley. They are included only where there is a known link with Radley going beyond their formal responsibility or where they raise other points of particular interest. They are always described as vicars of St Helen's so that this wider role is clear.

Building on an earlier list of incumbents drawn up by Radley History Club, extensive research was undertaken for this chapter, drawing in particular on the many resources that have since become available online. This produced more names and information. In some cases, however, it has not proved possible to confirm all this new information and thus guarantee its accuracy.

J. Standish *c.*1544

This name appears in the will of Thomas Porter of Thrupp in 1544. Thomas stated that he wanted his body to be buried within the Chapel of Radley before St John's [sic] altar and gave the high altar of the Chapel of Radley a bushel of barley. J. Standish was a legatee and was given 2s in the will to pray for Thomas's soul. However, an inventory of Thomas's goods, amounting to £52 14s 8d, shows that he had debts of over £29 to many people in the village and the church. He owed the Chapel of Radley £3 6s 8d and to 'Standysche, curate of Radley' the sum of 6s 8d.

Willielmus Cross (William Cross) *c.*1550

William Cross was a chaplain/curate at the Chapel of Radley in July 1550.

Sir John Gibbons *c.*1551-1553

John Gibbons was at the Chapel of Radley in May 1553. A comment attached to his record in the online Clergy of the Church of England Database indicates that his title was 'Sir'. He is also mentioned in the will of Richard Porter of Radley in 1551 as Sir John Gibbons, clerk curate.

Robertus Frauncys (Robert Francys) *c.*1554-1556

Robert Francys was instituted vicar of St Helen's Abingdon, which included the chapel at Radley, in March 1554 having been made a Fellow of All Souls College, Oxford, in 1541. Another record in February 1555 indicated that he was presented to Radley as a perpetual vicar but resigned in July 1556. He possibly became the vicar of Catherington in Hampshire in 1603.

Richard Cote *c.*1558

The 1558 will of Richard Sheen of Thrupp shows that the clerk curate of Radley witnessed it. Unfortunately his surname is not clear but it appears to be a word like Cote. Richard Sheen expressed a wish to be buried in the churchyard at Radley. He gave two bushels of wheat to the high altar of Radley Church and a quarter of barley to the church in Radley. He also gave two bushels of barley to the 'bell of Radley'.

Sir Randull Myllington c.1568

The will of John Crouch of Radley was witnessed in 1568 by Sir Randull Myllington as curate of the Church. Myllington received a bushel of wheat in the will.

Richard Mansell c.1586-1597

Richard Mansell was ministering to the parishioners of Radley in 1586. He held a stipendiary position in Radley in 1590, 1591 and 1595, and was a curate in 1597. His name appears as a witness to the will of Robert Sheene of Radley in 1596. On 23 November 1593, Letters of Administration of the will of Henry Butler of Radley were granted to Richard Maunsell of Radley, clerk, and Thomas Barnes of Radley, husbandman. In 1592/3 Richard Mansell witnessed the will of Amy Crouch of Radley. Three years later he witnessed the will of John Crouch, a yeoman of Radley.

Rodericus Lloid (Roderick Lloyd) c.1602-1612/3

Roderick Lloyd was the incumbent of Radley from about 1602 to 1612/3. It is thought to be his name carved on the outside of the south door of Radley Church (see Chapter 3).

The carving on the door of Radley Church 'Rodericus Lloid 1606'

Lloyd was buried at Radley on 21 March 1612/3. It would appear from his will that he was quite a wealthy man who had been able to lend money to parishioners and family. Like many others of this time, his will began with the fact that he was weak in body but of perfect memory. He commended his body to God and then continued to list the bequests he was making as follows:

> Towards the repair of Radley Church 2s 6d
>
> To the poor of the parish 10s to be distributed at the discretion of Thomas Shene and William Crouch
>
> To brother Howell £20 to be paid within one year after his decease
>
> To sister Ellen 20s
>
> To sister Gwen 20s and her children 10s apiece
>
> To brother Owen £20
>
> The legacies which his father gave him to be equally divided between the children of his brothers and sisters
>
> To his godson Lionel Crouch 40s and 12d apiece to his brothers and sisters
>
> To William [sic] his now wife 10s

> To his goddaughter Joan Barker 30s and her mother 10s
>
> To Alice Barker 5s
>
> To the rest of his godchildren 2s 6d apiece
>
> To Catherine Cox of Bayworth 10s
>
> To cousin Edward Evans of Woodstock 20s
>
> To Howell Meredith, two books which he now has
>
> To the poor of [?] 20s to be distributed at the discretion of the churchwardens
>
> To William Lewes 20s and to his sister Margaret 50s in gold
>
> To cousin Peter, 10s

All the rest of his goods and chattels, debts, bonds, bills, etc. he gave to his brother Hugh Lloyd who was the sole executor. He 'desired Theodore Price and William Barker to be overseers, and to have 10s apiece for their pains'.

Mr [illegible] principal of Harts Hall had a watch, which was to be delivered to Mistress Stonhouse, who was paying for the mending of it.

The following debts were stated in the will as owing to the testator:

> Mrs Nannby 40s
>
> Mrs Lewis for velvet 4s
>
> Mr Lewis of Sunningwell 40s
>
> Master Roderick Johnes 21s 6d
>
> Edward Baynes 52s 6d
>
> Brother Owen £80

Many in the parish owed him money and these debts were listed in a bill enclosed with the will. The rest of the debts were detailed in bonds and bills that, Lloyd says, could be found in his desk. His books, trunks and apparel were with William Croach [Crouch?] in Radley. He owed money to Prince, Barnes the mercer, Barker for shoes and Hugh the tailor.

Roderick Jones *c.*1612-1614

Roderick Jones graduated from Christ Church, Oxford, in 1605. He was ordained as a deacon in 1606 and three months later as a priest. He came to Radley in December 1612 and was 'licenced to serve the cure by Dr Marten' according to the Clergy of the Church of England Database. Henry Marten, Doctor of Law, was the Official of the Archdeacon of Berkshire at this time and dealt with granting probates and Letters of Administration.

Mention is given in the will of Roderick Lloyd of money owed by Master Roderick Johnes [Jones]. He was possibly a curate for Lloyd at a time when Lloyd's health was failing.

Jones was instituted as Rector of St Peter le Bailey in Oxford in 1614 but resigned in 1620.

John Vaughan *c.*1615-1618

There is conflicting evidence over John Vaughan's connection with Radley. On one hand, the note 'BT. Jo. Vaughan minister' appears at the end of the list of entries in the burial registers for Radley for 1615 to 1616 and 1617 to 1618. This may have been the John Vaughan who attended Jesus College, Oxford, was ordained a priest at Dorchester in 1614 and had previously been a deacon at Stanton Harcourt. On the other hand, a document headed 'Vicars' found among the diocesan papers at the Berkshire Record Office has the entry 'Mr Gifford Moyne (? vicar)' for 1615 to 1616 (see next entry).

Gifford Moyne *c.*1615-1616

As noted above, Gifford Moyne was possibly the incumbent at Radley in 1615 to 1616. The parish register for 1616 shows the baptism of Elizabeth Moyne, daughter of Mr Gifford [Clifford] Moyne and the baptism of a son, John, in 1615. However, the register does not have a title by his name as it does for Morgan Powell in 1620 (see next entry).

Morgan Powell *c.*1618–1625

Morgan Powell married Anne Sharp in Radley Church on 21 July 1618. From 1618 to 1620 he is described as a curate in the parish registers. He was called vicar in 1620, but this reverts to curate the following year. While he was in Radley it appears that four of his children were baptised at the Church: Ann in 1619, John in 1620, Elizabeth in 1622 and Morgan in 1624.

John Herbert *c.*1622-1668

Anthony à Wood wrote about John Herbert's student days in Oxford in *The History of Antiquities of the University of Oxford*. According to Wood, John Herbert was present at Broadgates Hall (the precursor to Pembroke College) in 1622 when Mr William Knight, a member of the College, preached in an apparently seditious way. Knight posed the question as to whether subjects in self-defence in the case of religion might take up arms against their sovereign and suggested that they could. After the service he was questioned by the Vice-Chancellor, Dr Piers, and was required to deliver up his notes. He was asked who had seen his notes before the service and one of the two people was John Herbert, named as vicar of Radley, near Abendon [sic]. The other man was John Code or Coode, like Herbert a student of Broadgates Hall. The Vice-Chancellor committed all three to prison. Knight was committed to the Gate House at Westminster. This all came to the attention of King James I, who was very grateful and commended the Vice-Chancellor for 'his discreet care in proceeding with that seditious preacher, Knight, as likewise in the commitment of those two other Masters of Arts, Herbert and Code'. The King also instructed the University to exclude the teachings of Jesuits and Puritans, as they 'meddled in the affairs of state and monarchy, and only preach Christ crucified'.

The Vice-Chancellor summoned all the heads of houses to his lodgings and read to them what the King had commanded them to do. William Knight had been basing his sermon on a tract by David Pareus, a German Protestant, so it was decreed that all books by him and those with a similar content should be burned. All libraries and bookshops were searched and the books were burned in St Mary's Churchyard on 6 June 1622. Burning of books also took place at Cambridge and London. Oxford University went further to detach itself from Knight's preaching by making all members subscribe to censures and decrees which prevented them from taking arms against the sovereign or making war against him. From that time onwards anyone taking a degree in any faculty had to take an oath to say that he condemned the doctrines of Pareus and that he would not preach, teach or maintain the same in the future.

According to Wood's book, when Herbert was released from prison he 'retired to his poor vicarage of Radley, near Abendon, where he lived until October 1668'. Herbert's protestant leanings did not appear to have an impact on Radley as the Compton Census of 1676 reported that the village had no non-conformists.

John Herbert married Joan Averie on 24 April 1628 but she died about two months later. He then married Judith (?) with whom he had six children (Judith, Sara, Katheren, Catheren, Elizabeth and Margaret) between about 1635 and 1648.

Although an educated man and a friend of the lord of the Manor, Sir William Stonhouse, Herbert had close links with the local farming community. He held 20 acres as a tenant of the lord of the Manor, although he may have sublet this holding rather than farmed it himself. His first wife was from a yeoman farming family (the Averies) and two of his daughters married into similar local families (the Elings and the Prettys). In Sir William's will dated January 1631/2 it says:

> I give to my friend Mr. John Herbert the one moiety of the Tithe White of Radley in as ample manner as is granted to me by the King's Letters Patent ALSO I give unto him Forty Shillings as a token of my love besides such duties belonging unto him by reason of his interest in the Tithes belonging to the Vicarage of Radley.

The witnesses to the will were John Herbert, vicar of Radley, John Curtaine and Ralfe Harper.

In the will of Sir William's wife, Dame Elizabeth Stonhouse, dated 20 January 1652/3 it says:

> I give to Mr John Herbert the now vicar of Radley forty shillings to be paid within one month after my interment which I desire may be performed by him in decent manner according to the established liturgy.

Dame Elizabeth seemed to want to make sure that the vicar performed the correct funeral service.

John Herbert was buried at Radley in October 1668. The transcriber of the parish registers noted that the year before his death the vicar's previously neat handwriting was wandering badly. Throughout 1668 it would appear that several people were responsible for filling in the burial register.

Little of the will left by John Herbert survives. However, the inventory which his wife, Judith, was asked to carry out and distribute 'as ordered by the bureaucrats' read thus:

Wearing apparel	£2.0.0
Books in his study	£5.0.0
Plate	£1.0.0
Chest of linen	£3.0.0
Four beds in several rooms	£5.0.0
Tubs and forms, stools and chairs in several rooms	£3.0.0
Pewter, brass and iron	£1.10.0
Wood and other lumber in the backside	£2.0.0
Sum	£22.10.0

These were very few possessions, even for a poor cottager at that time, and his poverty is in sharp contrast with the estate left by Roderick Lloyd shortly before (see entry above).

John's wife, Judith, died in 1707 and in her will she left her books to her grandsons, John Pretty, John Eling and Edward Eling, and goods in her chamber to her daughters Judith Saker, Sarah Pretty and Margaret Eling to be divided equally except for her woollen and linen apparel which was to be divided between Judith Saker and Margaret Eling. The money was divided equally among her seven grandchildren.

Edwardus Roode (Edward Roode) *c.*1624-1629

Edward Roode or Reede was appointed 'perpetual vicar' of St Helen's Abingdon and the Chapels of Radley and Drayton in 1624. He was deprived of his right to 'exercise the gifts and spiritual authority of God's word and sacraments conferred at ordination' in June 1629 as a result of the concerted efforts of the Mayott family of Abingdon who disapproved of him. However, he was reinstated in 1640 for three years.

A lecture at Abingdon School by its former headmaster, Michael St John Parker, in June 2006 about the relationship between Pembroke College, Oxford, and Abingdon School between 1624 and 1854 contains the following:

> In Abingdon, however, trouble was brewing. Edward Roode, Vicar of St Helen's since 1624, was preaching sermons, which denied the validity of the royal supremacy in religion, and the records of business in the Town Council show that there were bitter arguments between factions with opposing opinions about religion.

In 1610 Thomas Tesdale had bequeathed £5000 to enable boys from Abingdon School to receive an education at Oxford University. Richard Wightwick, Rector of East Ilsley, later increased this. Pembroke College, named after the Earl of Pembroke, came into being in 1624 for the purpose of educating 10 fellows and 10 scholars, all of whom had been educated at Abingdon School.

A biography of John Pendarvis by the Abingdon Area Archaeological and Historical Society notes that he came to Abingdon in 1644 with the parliamentary forces during the Civil War and was minister at St Helen's from about 1644 until 1649. It says:

> In the heated religious climate of the time, his position was as a Puritan who was more radical than the mainstream, but without being an extremist. St Helen's already had a nucleus of such believers thanks to its last pre-war vicar, Edward Roode.

William Carter 1668-1680

In a copy of a Terrier of the 'Holding, Tithes and other Dues belonging to the vicar of Radley, 8 April 1678', there is listed the Vicarage house and a little outhouse, orchard and garden, and 'all tithes of apples, nuts, eggs, hemp, pigs and cows'. It is signed by William Carter, Vicar, and Henry Nickolls and Richard Clinkard, churchwardens.

In the burial registers for Radley parish for 1680 there is a note stating that, 'Mr Curtyr (Carter) died in March 1680 and did not insert ye years burialls'.

John Winchurst 1681-1682

John Winchurst was the son of George Winchurst who was Abingdon's mayor in 1681. A certificate of residence of 1663 shows that a George Winchurst had an ironmonger's shop in Abingdon as well as an estate in Culham.

John matriculated in 1669 at the age of 16 and was a student at Pembroke College, Oxford. He spent a short time in Devon before coming to Radley. John died in September 1682 at the age of 29 and was buried in Radley on 14 November 1682. In the book, *The Life of Anthony Wood from the Year 1632 to 1672*, by Anthony Wood and Thomas Hearne there is the following information:

> 1682. Saturday at night died at Radley Mr John Winchurst MA and fellow of Pem. Coll. and Vicar at ------. At Radley buried in the Church 14, a good Scholar of a subtil head, a good mathematician born in Abendon, his father a maltster and mayor.

John Stonhouse 1683-1698

John Stonhouse received an MA from Oriel College, Oxford, and was ordained a priest in 1673 in Oxford. His name, as vicar, appears on the burial registers for Radley from 1683 to 1691. It is possible that he was a member of the Stonhouse family of the Manor of Radley but no evidence of this has been found.

In 1692 the Radley churchwardens' presentments to the diocese recorded that John Stonhouse had been reported for failing to preach every Sunday. At the same time Albon Bradshaw and his wife and Elizabeth Straford were reported for being recusants. The Bradshaws were again reported for recusancy in 1693 and for failing to pay the church rate for Church Farm in 1695. 'Recusants' was the term given to people who refused to conform to the Protestant Church of England. It is usually applied to Roman Catholics, with the term 'dissidents' being used for other groups such as Baptists and Methodists.

There is a death recorded for a Mr Jo. Stonhouse, son of Jos. Esq. in the Radley parish register in 1698.

Thomas Bayley 1699-1709

Between 1702 and 1705 some of the names in the parish register have the words 'Surveyed by Tho. Bayley' beneath them. However, it has been difficult to find details of who Thomas Bayley was. There was a Thomas Bayley who graduated with an MA from New Inn Hall, Oxford, and was ordained as a deacon at Christ Church Cathedral in Oxford in 1673. He was appointed in 1674 as a preacher in the diocese of Salisbury. He became a curate at Garford and Marcham, near Abingdon, in 1674 and it is possible that he took services at Radley during his time there but no evidence has been found to support this.

Nathaniel Thompson 1716-1745

Nathaniel was the son of William Thompson of London. Nathaniel's father has been described as a 'paynter and stayner' and on another occasion as a 'pictor'. When he died in 1710 it is said that he was doing work in St Paul's Cathedral. In the book *St Paul's: The Cathedral Church of London 604–2004* it says:

> During the second half of 1697 payments were made to John Moore and William Thompson for gilding mouldings, foliage in the frieze, palms and laurels and a 'glory' and also for painting the apse to look like veined marble and the four pilasters with gold-veined ultramarine.

According to *Cambridge University Alumni 1261-1900* Nathaniel was born on 24 April 1682 in London and attended Merchant Taylors' School in London. He was at Pembroke College, Cambridge, for some time and is thought to have matriculated at St John's College, Oxford, in 1702. He is mentioned in *The History of Merchant Taylors' School* by Harry Bristow Wilson as being the rector of Radley in the County of Berkshire at the presentation of Sir John Stonhouse, Bart, Rector of Sunningwell, Berks (1730-1746) and of Duns Tew, Oxon (1734). A Mrs Thompson was buried at Radley on 20 February 1757. Nathaniel died in August 1746 in Sunningwell.

Sir James Stonhouse 1754-1792

Sir James Stonhouse was the third son of Sir John Stonhouse of Radley Hall (see Chapter 1). He would not have expected to inherit the title and so, like many other younger sons, sought a profession. Sir John died in 1733 and was succeeded by his eldest son, also John. When he died unmarried in 1767, the title passed to his brother, William, who was also unmarried when he died in 1777. The title and Radley Hall thus passed to James, who died in 1792.

Sir James Stonhouse studied at St John's College, Oxford, becoming a Bachelor of Civil Law in 1742/3 and a Doctor of Civil Law in 1757. He was appointed rector of Sunningwell in 1746 under the patronage of his brother, Sir John. In 1753 Sir James resigned from Sunningwell and became rector of Clapham in Surrey. He held this position until his death in 1792 but, according to Francis Shepherd in his book, *London 1808-1870: The Infernal Wen,* the Revd Sir James Stonhouse 'had been an absentee … who had lived some forty years at his country estate near Oxford'; in his will made in 1783, Sir James states that he dwells in the Mansion House at Radley.

Sir James it appears was an example of what Shepherd refers to as the 'pluralism, absenteeism and clerical ignorance and indifference' that 'had become all too prevalent in the Church of England'. The extent to which he took services at Radley is not known; the list of Radley vicars from the Berkshire Record Office names Sir James as vicar with the note 'Jos. Benet curate'. This is likely to have been Joseph Benet, who was rector of Sunningwell from 1753 and 1796 and whose patron was Sir John Stonhouse, James's eldest brother.

Sir James Stonehouse, who was the 6th baronet of the 1670 creation and 9th baronet of the original creation (see Chapter 1 and Appendix 2), is sometimes confused with his cousin, also Revd Sir James Stonhouse, who succeeded to the title as the 10th baronet of the original creation and who practised for many years as a doctor before being ordained.

John Bradford 1792-1796

John Bradford is another whose name appears on the list of vicars from the Berkshire Record Office but for whom it has not been possible to find further information. There was a John Bradford who was a chaplain at Christ Church, Oxford, from 1789 to 1797 and this might be the person who took services at Radley.

John Lemprière 1796-1800

John Lemprière was born in about 1765 in Jersey. He was educated at Winchester College and Pembroke College, Oxford, and by 1803 had achieved his Doctor of Divinity degree. He was ordained as a priest in 1793, having been ordained as a deacon in 1788. In November 1788 he was receiving £50 per year from St Brelade's Church in Jersey where he was a curate. By 1794 he was classed as a lecturer or reader at St Nicolas', Abingdon.

Lemprière's career spanned various occupations. Around 1786 he started work on *A Classical Dictionary*, which contained a copious account of all the proper names mentioned in ancient authors and a chronological table of the value of coins, weights and measures used by the Greeks and the Romans. The book, published in 1788, proved popular but the time spent on it meant that Lemprière did not pay enough attention to his other duties.

Lemprière became assistant headmaster at Reading Grammar School in 1787 and a schoolmaster at Bolton Grammar School in 1791. He married Lucy Willince in 1790 in Reading. On the marriage certificate the address was given as St Aldate's, Oxford. The couple had 11 children between 1793 and 1807. There is an inscribed stone on the floor of St Nicolas' Church in Abingdon which records the death of his son John Francis in 1793 aged one month, his daughter Hellier in 1806 aged five months, and his daughter Jane in 1807 aged two years and ten months. Their mother, Lucy, was still alive in 1807, but must have died before 1813 when John married Elizabeth Deane in Caversham, near Reading, Berkshire. The couple had two children who survived. In April 1821, Trewman's *Exeter Flying Post* reported the death of Elizabeth at Shaldon 'in consequence of premature labour occasioned by fright'. In 1823, John married Ann Collingwood but died the following year in the Strand in London. It was reported that he died in a 'fit of apoplexy'.

In December 1796, according to Townsend's *History of Abingdon*, the vestry of St Nicolas' Church complained to the Bishop of Salisbury that evening prayers were not read daily according to John Blacknall's will and that Mr Lemprière, the curate, omitted the prayers sometimes on a Sunday morning in order to serve his curacy in Radley. Lemprière wrote to the Bishop saying he preferred the curacy in Radley, which he said was valued at £40 per year, presented by Sir George Bowyer, rather than 'an unsettled sermon of 10s 6d a Sunday'. The Bishop in his reply supported Lemprière and the trustees of St Nicolas' withdrew his salary. When he failed to get a stipend from St Nicolas' in 1799, Lemprière closed the church. It reopened when he became vicar of St Helen's in 1800.

For four years before becoming vicar of Abingdon in 1800, Lemprière was taking services at Radley. His capacity is not clear but there is some evidence that he was Radley's vicar during this period. This overlapped with his duties at Abingdon School (also known as Roysse's School), where he was headmaster from 1792. In *The Martlet and the Griffen – An Illustrated History of Abingdon School* by Thomas Hinde and Michael St John Parker, the authors state that Dr John Lemprière was:

> probably the finest scholar and the worst headmaster the school had ever had. He had a knack of securing clerical offices and at the time of his enforced resignation was receiving £98 10s 11d per annum and that was before he took on being vicar of St Helen's.

Falling numbers of pupils, which many people felt he had caused, led to his leaving Abingdon. Gradually the townspeople realised the seriousness of the situation at the school, forcing Lemprière's resignation. He resigned from Abingdon School in July 1810, having started at Exeter Free Grammar School in October 1809.

While at Abingdon it is said that he devised a money-making scheme to guarantee scholarships to his old College, Pembroke, in return for a payment of 20 guineas. His successor was not supposed to have any other job than that of headmaster, but this did not turn out to be the case and there was still controversy over the entry of Abingdon pupils to Pembroke College.

Lemprière's resignation as vicar from St Helen's Abingdon and the Chapels of Radley and Drayton took place in June 1811.

In 1819 he had a disagreement with the trustees of his new school because he had let the school fall into the same sorry mess that he had allowed Abingdon to get into. He was dismissed and he thought this was unfair. A report in the *Exeter Flying Post* of 10 July 1823 shows that he even petitioned Parliament about the manner in which he had been dismissed. It was referred to the Commissioners whose job it was to enquire into public charities. It seems that the dismissal was on the grounds that he was a corrupt influence. The House of Commons rejected his appeal for an inquiry. Mr Wilberforce presented another petition in the next session and the House of Commons decided that the grounds were completely false. There was some suggestion that the post had been given to a relative of one of the trustees, but the school was starting to flourish and it was decided that Lemprière was talented but did not have the correct character to be a headmaster.

Lemprière spent the rest of his life as a priest in Devon and is buried in Meeth. His appointment at Newton St Petrock carried with it a stipend of £160 per year; it is to be hoped the parishioners got their money's worth. Two of Lemprière's sons were also rectors of Meeth: Francis Drocus Lemprière (born 1794) and Everard Lemprière (born 1800).

Thomas Fry 1801-1803

When Thomas Fry married Miss Cresswell, the daughter of Estcourt Cresswell of Bibury, Gloucestershire, in September 1802 in Oxford he was described in *Jackson's Oxford Journal* as a Fellow of Lincoln College, Oxford, and the vicar of Radley. He was appointed a rector of Emberton in 1804 and a stipendiary curate in Hardmead in 1814. In *A Biographical Dictionary of the Living Authors of Great Britain and Ireland,* 1814, it is written:

> Rev. Thomas Fry MA formerly tutor of Lincoln College, Oxford
>
> He entered upon the clerical function at Abingdon; afterwards became curate at Hanwell, when he removed to Lock Chapel in 1803. Having relinquished the chaplaincy, he now retains only the living of Emberton, Bucks; but is reported to be designed to fill the office of Minister of Christianity to the Jews, in the chapel, which the London Society is proceeding to erect for this purpose, within the pale of the Church of England.

Thomas Fry contributed to the Christianity to the Jews Society until 1811 when he retired to his parish at Emberton.

Edward Lewton 1803-1805

Edward Lewton's name appears in the list compiled by Revd Allso in his book and on the list of vicars at Radley found among the diocesan papers at the Berkshire Record Office with, in brackets, 'T. Stonhouse Vigor. assists. 1805'; Timothy Stonhouse Vigor was rector of Sunningwell from 1796 to 1812 and a son of the Revd Dr Sir James Stonhouse (see above). However, the only Edward Lewton it has been possible to trace was an MA from Wadham College, Oxford, who was ordained by the Bishop of Oxford in 1793 and appointed a public preacher before the University in 1804. From 1806 until his death in 1830, he was a classical and general literature professor at the East India College, which had been set up to train administrators of the East India Company.

Kenneth McKenzie Reid Tarpley 1806-1807

Born about 1781, Kenneth McKenzie Reid Tarpley was the incumbent at Radley for about a year in 1806. Like Lemprière, Tarpley was born in Jersey. He was ordained in 1805 and instituted vicar at St Mary Magdalen in Oxford in 1808. Nothing is known about his time in Radley, but after leaving the village, his life was not without controversy. The following resumés of legal cases involving Tarpley are included to give some idea of his character. Radley was probably lucky to only have his services for a short time!

In 1815 Tarpley became vicar of Floore. In 1821, a young woman called Susan Swadlin was awarded damages of £50 for defamation of character by Mrs Tarpley. Revd Tarpley wrote in *The Times* in August 1821 that Susan had been one of their servants but had turned out to have a most vile character and so he had given her a very poor reference. The judge felt that he had gone much further in this than he should go, that it was very malicious and that he had been actuated by vindictive feelings. Many people in Oxford where Susan had worked previously came to her defence and the Tarpleys lost the case.

In 1833, the jury in another case returned a verdict for the plaintiff, the 15-year-old son of K.M.R. Tarpley and awarded him damages of a farthing. The son had allegedly been trying to take down a poster put up by a wealthy landowner, Mr Back, when the man's groom assaulted him. This incident occurred when the vicar's son was returning late one evening from bat fowling (catching roosting birds at night). The evidence was poor and the judge felt that the case should never have been brought to court. There appears to have been a substantial disagreement between Mr Back and the Revd Tarpley. This was compounded when the vicar tried to lead a group over the landowner's land, which they felt they had the right to do. A very acrimonious fight ensued.

In 1833 the *Leicester Chronicle* wrote that the reverend gentleman should 'act in a more peaceable manner towards a Mr Humfrey of the village of Floore'. In court, Tarpley was bound over to keep the peace in relation to this. The reporter commented that 'the village of Floore had for a length of time been disturbed and embroiled by the disgraceful practices of some of its inhabitants'.

In November 1833 the *Morning Post* wrote:

> Sir J. Scarlett moved to file a 'criminal information' against Rev. K.M. Tarpley, a clergyman and magistrate of the county of Northampton, for riotous and violent conduct towards Mr Back, a gentleman residing near Mr Tarpley's vicarage. The affidavit on which the application was made imputed to the Rev. gentleman an attempt to force a right of way over the pleasure grounds of Mr Back, and improper conduct in meeting persons who had been convicted under the Trespass Act, to aid and encourage them in their riotous intentions.
>
> The court having heard the affidavit refused to grant a rule, observing that it was open to the party to proceed by indictment.

In reply to this, Tarpley put a notice in the local paper denying the allegations and said that the magistrates had dismissed the case against him, his son and the five labourers alluded to in the application. He stated that legal proceedings were pending which would fully justify him.

In December 1835 the plaintiff, Tarpley, obtained a verdict against a farmer, Mr Blaby, in the parish of Floore for a series of libels published in the *Northampton Free Press* in 1832 against him. The farmer had placarded the village with such posters as 'Cut-free Tarpley', 'Church mouse Tarpley' and 'Tarpley the dog killer'. These placards had been the result of a village feud and the object had been to bring the plaintiff into disgrace and to banish him from society altogether. It did not help that Tarpley was a Tory and Blaby was a Whig, and party politics exacerbated the situation. The defendant claimed that Tarpley had been equally malicious and that he put the job of vicar low down on his priorities, but the jury decided in favour of Tarpley and awarded damages of 40s. Blaby was refused leave to appeal against the ruling in 1836.

In 1837 Tarpley was in the debtors' court for being insolvent to the amount of £5,000. He blamed the court cases he had been involved in for this and the fact that his stipend at Floore had been £500 per year but his living had been sequestrated and his income had been reduced to £150. He was given 10 weeks' imprisonment from the date of his petition for a 'vexatious defence of the action'. He was discharged from the Fleet prison in London on 22 April 1837. In January 1842 he applied to be discharged from his debt but the case was adjourned. A few weeks later he was discharged.

In June 1838 the churchwardens in Floore brought a case against him for 'spoliation of the churchyard wall'. This appeared to relate to the problems of right of way and the Vice-Chancellor's court directed that the existence of a right of way or no right of way should be ascertained first.

According to the 1851 Census, Tarpley was living as a curate at the vicarage in Kensworth, in Hertfordshire. In 1861, aged 79, he was lodging at the home of a Mary Ann Brewitt in Marylebone, London. He died in 1865 in the St Pancras District of London.

John Radcliffe 1807-1852

John Radcliffe gained a BA degree from St Mary Hall, Oxford, in February 1807. The same month he became curate at Radley. His ordination as a priest took place in 1808 and sometime later he was awarded an MA. After this he was referred to as vicar. During his time as vicar of Radley, Radcliffe was also a precentor of Christ Church, Oxford, and vice-principal of St Mary Hall.

According to Parliamentary papers published in 1818, John Radcliffe contributed information to the Select Committee on Education of the Poor, etc. He reported that the population of Radley at that time was 337 and that Henry Bellairs was his curate (see entry below). His report said that there were:

> Two Sunday schools at Radley, consisting of 21 boys and 25 girls and one at Kennington containing 20 girls and 10 boys. The whole was supported by voluntary contributions.

Radcliffe observed that the poor would be very glad to have the means of education. He also noted that, while the parents of some of the children were dissenters, they never objected to their children learning the catechism and attending divine service at the established church.

In 1827 when Radley Hall was occupied by a school (Radley House Seminary) run by Benjamin Kent, Radcliffe attended an entertainment there. He did not like what he saw from the religious point of view. Benjamin Kent later became a Baptist minister and while headmaster had already shown his leanings towards the dissenters. Kent's school closed in 1844 and the buildings were rented in 1847 to Revd William Sewell and Robert Corbet Singleton who had been inspired by the Oxford Movement in the Anglican Church. They founded a boys' school, St Peter's College, later known as Radley College (see Chapter 1). Radcliffe showed distaste for the new school because he thought that it had leanings towards Papism. Hostility developed between Radcliffe and the College's founders.

Singleton wrote a diary which is published on the Radley College website. For 11 April 1847 he wrote about his plans to rent the house and land from the Bowyer family:

> Mr Bowyer recommended us to go to Dr Radcliffe, the vicar, who resides in Holywell Street, Oxford, and tell him about our plan – a reasonable suggestion. He said we should find him a gentleman, a scholar, and a good churchman. This gives us hope that we shall get on very well with him.

On 26 April 1847 Singleton wrote:

> Sewell went to Dr Radcliffe this morning, who received him stiffly enough. The old gentleman seemed to have a thorough horror of anything approaching to a school; and not without some reason; for it appears that the last tenant of Radley Hall was a schoolmaster, whose boys, if not himself, were chiefly dissenters and caused the vicar very much annoyance.

Writing in the diary on 9 June 1847 about a service for St Columba's Day, Singleton said:

> Mr Radcliffe, the vicar of Radley, has not yet called, which extraordinary as it is, is very convenient; for we should not at all have relished his company, and yet we could scarce have avoided asking him, had he been civil.

Singleton observed in his diary that both he and Sewell had tried to make friendly advances towards Radcliffe but they had been rejected. The staff and pupils at Radley College attended Radley Church until they had a chapel of their own. Singleton reported that they had to contend with:

> Mr Radcliffe's irreverence, the scandalous singing, the uncertainty of hours – the women, both inside and outside, staring at the boys – and so on.

When the College Chapel got its licence, which Radcliffe had to approve, the sub-warden 'found the old gentleman wonderfully civil'. Singleton wished to have Holy Communion once a month in the College Chapel but the Bishop suggested it should be more often. Singleton was probably eager to point out that Mr Radcliffe celebrated it once per quarter.

Bishop Wilberforce kept a diary with some rather frank comments about the local clergy. On Radcliffe he said:

Many good points about him. Spent more always than gets. Not a man one would choose. Late Vice Principal of St Mary Hall.

The Norman font in Radley Church, which had lain buried and hidden in a shed at Church Farm probably since the Civil War, was reinstated in Radley Church in 1840 at the instigation of John Radcliffe (see Chapter 3).

Radcliffe lived in Oxford at least for the latter part of his ministry. It is said that he made the journey to and from Radley on foot, resting on the way to enjoy a pipe of tobacco with the result that the time of his arrival could vary considerably. In the 1851 Census, he is recorded as being born in Rochdale and living at 96 Holywell Street, Oxford, with his widowed sister-in-law, Mary Radcliffe, a gentlewoman (his sister who died in *c.*1828 was also called Mary). His occupation was given as a Chaplain of Merton College. The household had two servants. In the 1841 Census he was also recorded living with his sister-in-law and they had three boys living with them, two aged 10 and one aged eight.

According to *Jackson's Oxford Journal*, John Radcliffe died in February 1852 from disease of the heart at his residence in Holywell Street, Oxford. He was said to be vicar of Radley, Chaplain of Merton College and the Radcliffe Infirmary, and formerly vice-principal of St Mary Hall. He was aged 70 and was buried at Radley. There is a plaque on the south wall of Radley Church (see Chapter 3) which says:

In memory of the Rev[D] John Radcliffe M.A. for more than 40 years vicar of this parish.

He was found dead with a prayer book in his hand February 21 1852.

Be ye also ready for in such an hour as ye think not the son of man cometh.

In the same vault rests the body of his only sister Mary Radcliffe who died unmarried 24 years before.

Thomas Hinde 1813

Thomas Hinde, born about 1787, is recorded in the parish registers as the officiating minister at the funeral in Radley of John Howse aged 14 months. He was a chaplain at Christ Church, Oxford, from 1812 to 1825 and administered some of the services at Radley. He was vicar of Featherstone in Yorkshire from 1825 until his death in 1874.

Charles Boothby 1816

Charles Boothby was a stipendiary curate at Radley in 1816. His stipend was £30 per year and he was permitted to reside at Oxford, four miles away, so he could pursue his studies at the university. Charles was the son of William Boothby of Dublin. He attended St Mary Hall, Oxford, and matriculated in 1815 with his ordination as a priest taking place a year later. He gained his BA in 1819. Prior to this he had been a captain of engineers in the army and lost a leg at Talavera (near Madrid) in 1809 in the Spanish Peninsular War. In 1819 he became vicar of Sutterton in Lincolnshire and in 1829 he was a canon at Southwell in the Canonry and Prebend of North Muskham. In 1831 he was at Bleasby, Nottinghamshire with a stipend of £90 per year. He was in the York jurisdiction of Bishop Edward Venables Vernon Harcourt and was the domestic chaplain of Thomas Henry Liddell, 1st Baron Ravensworth.

Henry Bellairs 1817-1819

According to the Clergy of the Church of England Database, Henry was the son of Abel Walford Bellairs of Stamford in Lincolnshire. We are also informed that Henry was a midshipman in the Royal Navy and was wounded at the Battle of Trafalgar in 1805. Afterwards he was in the 15th Hussars. He was obviously a late entrant to St Mary Hall, Oxford, as he matriculated in 1816 at the age of 25. Henry was a stipendiary curate at Radley in 1817. Like Charles Boothby he was allowed to live in Oxford and had the same stipend. The reason given for his not living at Radley Vicarage was that it was 'deemed unfit'. In 1818, a year after he was ordained, he was a priest at the Quebec Chapel in St Marylebone in London. In 1819 he went to Bedworth as a stipendiary curate where he was receiving £150 per year, plus a further £50 and use of the rectory house. He received his MA in 1823 and left Bedworth in 1832 to become vicar of Hunsingore. He was an Honorary Canon at Worcester in 1853 and died in 1872.

Henry's wife was Dorothy Parker McKenzie. Their third son Charles was baptised at Radley in 1818 and, like his father, took Holy Orders.

Notes in the burial register for 1813 to 1826 show that the Revd Henry Bellairs presented 14 octavo prayer books and 48 Ludivine [sic] prayer books to the parish. He was repaid by subscriptions from the Revd John Radcliffe and Revd Charles Boothby. Charles Bishop, Reginald Pole and John Hinckley also subscribed and the total amount came to £7 4s 0d.

Mr Townsend 1819

Jackson's Oxford Journal for 26 June 1819 states that the curate of Radley, a Mr Townsend, had given two guineas to the Wantage District Committee for the Deanery of Abingdon. Mr Radcliffe, the vicar, gave £1.

William Beadon Heathcote 1852

William Heathcote

When John Radcliffe died, William Beadon Heathcote succeeded him for a short time as vicar of Radley. Heathcote, a friend of the Sewell family at Radley College, had been a scholar at Winchester and later a fellow and tutor at New College, Oxford. He became sub-warden of New College in 1840 and warden of Radley College following the retirement of Singleton in 1851. When he took on the post he was not aware of the precarious financial position the College faced. He brought in some very useful reforms in the short time he was warden but resigned at the end of 1852. When Heathcote wished to get married, the College rules had to be changed to allow a married man to hold the post of warden. He married Elizabeth Mary Deane, daughter of Revd George Deane, vicar of Bighton, Hampshire, on 3 August 1852 and they had a daughter, Agnes Mary, in 1854. Their son Cecil Hamilton Heathcote died in Ceylon aged 39 in 1895. He was a telephone engineer.

William was born in about 1813, the son of the Venerable Gilbert Heathcote and Anne Beadon. He was a Fellow of New College from 1832 to 1853. In June 1854 he became precentor of Salisbury Cathedral and then vicar of Sturminster Marshall in Dorset from 1858 to 1862. Following this he moved to become rector of Compton Bassett in Wiltshire, but died that year in London where he had gone to seek medical treatment.

In a religious census return of 1852, the vicar, either William Beadon Heathcote or John Radcliffe, wrote that there had been a Sunday school belonging to the Established Church in Radley since 1807. It was held in a separate building near the Church and there were 40 scholars, none of whom paid or provided their own books. At that time 12 of these children were attending a day school. At the Sunday school, where only reading and religious knowledge were taught, there were three unpaid female teachers and one paid male teacher.

Robert Gibbings 1853-1865

Robert Gibbings was born in about 1820 at Charleville, County Cork, Ireland. In 1846, when Sewell and Singleton, the founders of Radley College resigned from St Columba's College in Ireland, one of the people who came to England with them was Robert Gibbings. Another was E.G. Monk (see Chapter 3 and the entry below for George Wharton).

Robert Gibbings came from an ecclesiastical family. His father was Revd Thomas Gibbings, a vicar at Ballingarry in County Limerick from 1821 to 1839. Robert's many siblings included the Revd Richard Gibbings, who was Professor of Ecclesiastical History at Trinity College Dublin. His paternal grandfather was Revd Richard Gibbings of Gibbings Grove, Charleville, in County Cork.

Robert had been a fellow at St Columba's College in Ireland but, on coming to England, he became a curate at Peasemore, near Wantage. On St Columba's Day in June 1847, he went to Radley College and, according to Singleton in his diary, sat himself in a position which looked as if he was one of their fellows. He indicated to Singleton that he would like to be one but he received the reply that 'Providence had designed him for another sphere'. He returned to his parish that evening.

On the day of the opening of Radley College in August 1847, Gibbings went with a friend, Mr Forbes, a relative of his rector's wife. Singleton wrote in his diary that Gibbings had told him that the vicar of Radley (John Radcliffe) had written to the Rector of Stackallen in Ireland, where they had come from, for a reference to the character of Singleton and Monk. Singleton felt that they must be 'a pretty black couple' in Radcliffe's eyes, but decided that they would go on treating the vicar with respect and that if the vicar continued to be hostile then it would be his fault.

During 1848 Sewell was keen for Gibbings to be a fellow at Radley College, but Gibbings was worried about leaving his curacy. He went back to Ireland to consult his father, who had not been keen on his working at St Columba's College but gave his consent for Gibbings to work at Radley College. Singleton wrote in his diary on 10 September 1848:

> This rejoiced us all greatly; for he is so amiable, cheerful, and good tempered, – also a good scholar, a priest, and a gentleman, that I am sure he will be a great addition to our Society, – and thus all who seceded from St Columba's have, by a curious combination

of circumstances, been brought together at St Peter's. Thus if we were driven away from an employment, to which we were all heartily devoted, Providence has united us again in a similar work, under far higher auspices, unembarrassed by a thousand difficulties which thwarted us in Ireland, and in every possible way far superior. May God make us thankful and earnest.

When Sewell took over as warden at Radley College in 1853 following Singleton's resignation, Robert Gibbings became a teacher at the College and also the vicar of Radley Church. He married Caroline Stockdale (formerly Irby) in 1859 and they had three daughters of whom two, Agnes Fanny and Caroline Mary, were baptised in Radley.

Jackson's Oxford Journal reported that Gibbings' sudden death in January 1865 came as a shock to the villagers. Although he had complained of a little indisposition, he had been carrying out his duties and had not thought it necessary to seek medical advice. At four o'clock during the night in which he died, his wife had called the housekeeper to light a fire in the dressing room and send for Mr Stone, the surgeon. Within a short time the vicar had died and Mrs Gibbings fainted. Mr Stone told the inquest jury that there was nothing to suppose that the death was other than by natural causes. He had no doubt that a vessel in the heart had given way. In the February following his death the household furniture, pony, carriage, harness and effects, including a walnut whatnot and greenhouse plants, were sold by auction at the Vicarage.

Mrs Gibbings gave birth to their third daughter, Emma, on 31 August 1865 in Northamptonshire, seven and a half months after her husband had died. She was aged about 40 at the time and this had been her second marriage.

William Henry Ranken 1865-1867

At this time the Radley Church living was 'donative', with the right of appointment held by the Bowyer family. But when a new vicar needed to be appointed in 1865 following the sudden death of Revd Gibbings, the current holder of the Bowyer baronetcy could not do so because he was a Roman Catholic. The appointment was instead made by the University of Oxford. The recipient was the Revd William Henry Ranken, who had twice been a fellow of Radley College and was then the vicar of Sandford-upon-Thames. He became sub-warden of the College in 1867. Before he left Sandford Church, Ranken paid almost the total cost of its extension and restoration.

Ranken was born in about 1833 in Brislington, Somerset, to Charles (born in Ireland) and Isabella Ranken. In 1851 he was a scholar at Corpus Christi College, Oxford. He matriculated in 1850 aged 17 and received his MA in 1857, becoming a fellow in 1862 until 1869. Ranken travelled around quite a bit. In 1861 he was a curate in East Retford, Nottinghamshire, living with his sister, Isabella. He was vicar of Sandford-upon-Thames from 1862 to 1867, a period which partly overlapped with his time at Radley. He was vicar of West Houghton, Lancashire, from 1868 to 1869 and Maisey-Hampton, near Cricklade, in Gloucestershire from 1869 to 1884. He was vicar of Surbiton in Surrey from 1884 to 1901and then rector of

Byfield in Northamptonshire from 1901 to 1919. Ranken married Frances Mary Casson, 11 years his junior, in 1869 in Ffestiniog, Merionethshire. He died on 11 November 1920.

William Wood 1868-1870

William Wood

William Wood, the then warden, was appointed as vicar by Radley College which by then had purchased the right to make the appointment from the Bowyer family; the dispute with the Bishop of Oxford is described earlier in the chapter.

After Radley, Wood went to Cropredy near Banbury, where he remained for almost 30 years. He was rector of Monks Risborough in Buckinghamshire from 1898 to 1901, and then vicar of Rotherfield Greys in Oxfordshire. He died aged 90 in 1919 at Greys Rectory.

Born in about 1829 in Rochdale, Lancashire, Wood married Emma Moorsom in Brighton in 1862. They had eight children: Kenneth Forbes (*c.*1864), Michael H.M. (*c.*1865), Cyril Edward (*c.*1866), Cicely Frances Ouseley (*c.*1867), Robert Moorsom (1869), Francis Ludlow (1870), Sylvia M. (1872) and Dorothea Mary (1875). Cicely, Robert and Francis were born while he was at Radley College.

Edward Barber 1868-1883

Edward Barber was the curate at Radley Church from about 1868 to 1883, during the whole of the incumbency of William Wood and Charles Martin, and part of the incumbency of Robert James Wilson, who were all in turn wardens of Radley College. Edward Barber was appointed a master at Radley College in 1868 and lived in Radley's newly extended vicarage (see Chapter 2).

Edward Barber

Barber was born in about 1842 in Brighouse, Yorkshire. He married Edith Sarah Evetts in Wycombe District in 1869. She was born in Iffley, near Oxford. Their sons Edward, Arthur William and Cyril Frederick were baptised at Radley in 1870, 1873 and 1876 respectively.

Barber appears to have had quite a lot of contact with the village school and encouraged the children to attend regularly by giving out small amounts of money according to how well they had attended. During Barber's term of office at Radley the village school was replaced by a new building. Sarah Jones became the new head teacher of Radley Primary School at the beginning of 1873 and her first entry in the school's log book said that it was the first day in the new building. Revd Barber visited the school that day to welcome her. Two weeks later he entertained the children for tea and in the evening he amused them with a magic lantern show in the schoolroom.

On leaving Radley in 1883, Edward and his wife were presented with several gifts. *Jackson's Oxford Journal* recorded the presentation and noted that he was the 'esteemed vicar of the village and Inspector of Schools for the Diocese of Oxford'. The main present was a cathedral-toned clock in a case of unpolished walnut, very richly decorated with six inlaid gilt plates, each embellished with picturesque rural scenery in permanent colours. The couple also received a set of silver plated entrée dishes, and a pocket Communion service was presented to the vicar. The school children presented him with a 'chastely-decorated oak ink stand'. Mrs Barber received a 'massive plain polished gold bracelet'. Mr G.H. Osmond, an Oxford jeweller, supplied the items.

For a short time after leaving Radley, Barber became the rector of Chalfont St Giles. He then went to Chester, living there until his death in 1914. In the 1911 Census Edward is recorded as an archdeacon living with his wife at St Bridget's Rectory in Chester.

Charles Martin 1871-1879

The Revd Charles Martin was born in Staverton, Devon, in about 1841. He became a student at New College, Oxford, then senior student and tutor at Christ Church, Oxford. He was an assistant master at Harrow School (1869 to 1870) before being elected warden at Radley College in 1870. Warden Martin was appointed vicar of Radley Church by Radley College although his curate, Edward Barber, carried out most of his duties.

Charles Martin

In *No Ordinary Place, Radley College and the Public School System 1847-1997*, Christopher Hibbert wrote that Charles Martin was 'a scholar, a lover of music and an enthusiastic cricketer, Martin was a considerate man and a thoughtful one'. Charles Martin married Dora Frances Moberly in 1869 and they had nine children between 1870 and 1882. Unfortunately Martin did not have a very successful career at Radley College and he left to take up a living in Norfolk. He then went to Dartington Rectory in Devon, where he died in 1910 at the age of about 69.

Humphrey Fleming Pinder 1874-1876

In 1874 *Jackson's Oxford Journal* announced that Mr Pinder had been licensed to the curacy of Radley. Humphrey Fleming Pinder was born in Bratton Fleming in 1852 and attended Marlborough College before going to Cambridge University. He was an assistant master at Radley College from 1873 to 1879 and during this time was a curate of Radley Church. He became a curate in Witney in 1881 and later headmaster of Witney Grammar School. While in Witney he married Katherine Isabel Neate in 1913. He died in 1916 in Wolverhampton.

George Wharton 1876-1883

George Wharton was born in about 1840 in Kinver, Staffordshire, where his father, also called George, was vicar. In the 1851 Census, at the age of 12, he is recorded as being educated at home with his two sisters and a brother by an assistant tutor who lived with them.

Wharton was curate at Radley from 1876 to 1883, but was involved with Radley Church for a longer period. He became a fellow and precentor at Radley College in 1862, and remained there until his death on 23 December 1925. His effects amounted to just over £7,000 and administration of his will was granted to Eleanor Maud Augusta Palin, a widow.

George Wharton

Robert Sephton, a member of Radley History Club, has researched Wharton's life. He writes of him:

> He was said to be without exceptional musical talent, but he was a competent organist and became a successful choirmaster as well as teaching mathematics and other subjects to the lower forms. Under him, the organ was transferred to the new chapel of Thomas Graham Jackson when it was brought into use in 1895. He organised secular concerts – he was a Gilbert & Sullivan fan – to which the villagers were invited for the dress rehearsals.

Although remembered by Radleians as a clergyman, he was not ordained until about 1874, having had difficulty in passing the ordination examination. After Edward Barber's departure in 1883, he was called upon to resume some parish duties for periods up to 1891 and beyond, although he had noted in his diary that he preached his last sermon as curate in the Church in May 1883. He would have been familiar to the villagers, taking his parish duties conscientiously and adding visiting to the many duties he took on in the College. In his unpublished diaries Wharton noted how the lack of sanitation and the dampness of the village's little black and white cottages kept the death rate high and him busy with burials. He visited a Mrs Badnall who was in a dying state and a girl called East who was the daughter of the College gas man. He officiated at the funeral of Mrs Hepzibah Crutch who died aged 47 by throwing herself out of a window and was present when his fellow curate, Edward Barber, officiated at the funeral of Sir George Bowyer who died in 1883 and, despite being a Roman Catholic, was buried in the family vault in Radley churchyard.

He was remembered for the sermons he preached for which he had a unique style of delivery. They were well arranged, intelligible and scriptural, and it was remarked that they hardly ever failed to consign some part of the congregation to hell.

George Wharton kept in touch with people outside the College. These included Lord Berkeley on Boars Hill and the Dockar-Drysdales at Wick Hall. He visited interesting buildings and fashionable seaside resorts including the 'pleasing town of Southport with its disappointing beach'. In Blackpool in 1908 he rode on the scenic railway. The Prince of Wales was his contemporary at Magdalen College, Oxford, and when the Prince opened its new library he mentioned how pleased he was to see Wharton again. Another royal connection was when Wharton sang and played at one of Lady Affleck's parties the night before the Prince Consort died and the Prince of Wales turned the pages for him. In 1903 he was able to give the opening recital on the new organ in the

Parish Church erected by public subscription in memory of his predecessor [as precentor] at the College, Dr Edwin George Monk.

Wharton was interested in conjuring and in supernatural appearances and following on from this he attempted to give credence to the story that Admiral Sir George Bowyer could still be heard stomping on the stairs with his wooden leg. He also claimed to have seen an apparition of a monk beside him when playing the organ and on another occasion when he was leaving the Chapel at night.

He assembled a collection of antiques of all kinds – silver, china, furniture, snuff boxes and even pseudo-Elizabethan chairs. His most treasured item, for which he was noted, was a watch, which chimed the hours and quarters. On a more solemn note, he later assembled a collection of photos of students killed in the First World War.

Revd Roscoe Beddoes, who was a pupil at Radley College when Wharton died, wrote an affectionate *Memoir* of him in which he remarks that:

> He marched along piously and happily, strong in the best tradition of Queen Victoria, certain that all was for the best in the best of all worlds.

Wharton remained in post as precentor until he was 76 in 1914 and continued to have a College room until his death in 1925. He is buried in Radley churchyard with an inscription over his grave recalling his duties as precentor, which reads, 'He set singers before the Lord'. A music prize at the College was founded in his honour in 1913.

Robert James Wilson 1880-1893

Robert James Wilson was the last of the three vicar wardens, being appointed in 1880. He was formerly an assistant master (1863 to 1866) at Radley College, then an assistant master at Marlborough College (1866 to 1870), a tutor at Merton College, Oxford (1870 to 1875) and vicar of Wolvercote (1875 to 1879). Despite leaving Radley College in 1888 to become warden of Keble College, Oxford, he remained vicar of Radley until 1893 in order for negotiations to be completed with Miss Bowyer in 1892 for the permanent right of presentation of the incumbent.

Robert Wilson

Wilson died on 15 May 1897. He had been unwell for some time, but had continued with his work until he was struck down with a brain haemorrhage. The Revd James Nash (see entry below) wrote in the parish magazine that Radley had lost a friend. Wilson had welcomed the children of Radley to go and play in Keble College quad on various occasions and to listen to a wonderful musical box being played. He was buried in the cemetery of Holywell, Oxford.

Wilson wrote *The Catholic Church* and the *Church of Rome* and was joint author with Canon Liddon of *The Life of Dr Pusey*.

During his time as vicar, Wilson was assisted in his duties by a succession of curates, some of whom are referred to in parish records as the 'priest in charge'. As can be seen below, some of these curates stayed only a short time.

J.N. Doran 1881

Doran is referred to as the priest-in-charge when burials were recorded in 1881.

Alfred Herbert Stanton 1883-1886

Stanton became the curate of Radley in 1883, but after three years moved to Llangasty Tal-y-llyn in Brecon. In 1896, after being in Bournemouth for a year, he became the rector of Hambleden near Henley, Oxfordshire. Stanton wrote a book entitled *On Chiltern Slopes: The Story of Hambleden*, and co-authored and revised a book entitled *St Peter in the East, Oxford*.

Stanton was born in about 1856 in Farmington, Gloucestershire. He married his cousin Edith Eleanor Cripps in Henley in 1883 and in 1884 a daughter, Mary Katherine, was born. Hilda Edith was born in about 1885 and Rosa Grace was born in about 1889. Stanton died in December 1946 in Oxford where he had been living since he retired. He was laid to rest in Hambleden, where he had been rector until 1924. Revd Pixell (see entry below) commented in the *Radley News* in 1947 that he was a great saint and it had been a privilege to know him. Pixell had visited him several times in Oxford and found him 'practically helpless and, at the end, bedridden but was always very patient'.

Arthur Warcup Malim 1886-1887

Arthur Malim was born in about 1843 in Higham Ferris, Northamptonshire, where his father was vicar. Malim was the priest-in-charge at Radley under Warden Wilson between 1886 and 1887. He married Jane Dandridge, who was born in East Hendred, at Radley Church in 1888 when she was a spinster of 46 and he was a bachelor aged 45. By this time he was resident in Stowe, Northamptonshire. In 1871 he was the curate of Peasemore, near Wantage, and was curate of Kelsale, Suffolk, from 1880 to 1883.

Malim died on 17 November 1892 at Hampton Lucy. Jane died in 1913. After Arthur's death she lived at 'The Home' in Clifton Hampden near Abingdon. In the 1901 Census she is identified as the lady superintendent at a home of rest at that residence with her niece, Irene M. Badcock, as her assistant. The magnificent reredos in Radley Church (see Chapter 3) was presented by Jane in 1910 in memory of her husband.

Hugh Francis Williams 1888

Hugh Francis Williams was born in about 1853 in London and studied at Oxford. He is recorded as officiating at burials in Radley in 1888. The Census records show that he was a clergyman and assistant master at St John's College, Hurstpierpoint, in 1881. In 1891, the year he died, he was a boarder at 2 Oakley Court in London. His father Albert was an attorney and solicitor who was born in East Ilsley in Berkshire.

William James Stavert 1888

Stavert was a curate at Radley. He was born in Lytham St Annes, Lancashire, in about 1868 and studied at Cuddesdon Theological College near Oxford. Following his time in Radley he became rector of Burnsall in Yorkshire. Stavert married Alice Mary Coverley in 1902 and died in 1932.

John William Kempe 1889-1890

Kempe was another curate of Radley. In 1881 he was assistant curate of St John the Divine, Kennington in London and Chaplain of Stockwell Hospital. He was single and was born in Leeds, Yorkshire, in about 1834. In the 1891 Census he was living at the rectory in Hockliffe, Bedfordshire, with a housekeeper and one servant. He died in 1903.

In the Radley parish registers there is a note that reads:

> 10 April 1889
>
> East. Ellen Agnes Ann. Baptised by R.W. East in case of judged necessity – the child only survived the baptism by a few minutes. I had urged the parents to bring the child to baptism but they delayed until it was too late.
>
> J.W. Kempe, Priest

George F. Driver 1891-1892

The 1891 Census shows that George F. Driver was living with his wife who was about 12 years his senior, at the vicarage in Radley. He was born in about 1845 in Bridgwater, Somerset, and became a curate at Dodington, Shropshire. In 1881 he was the curate of West Kirby Church in Cheshire. While there he married Catherine Ann Barker in 1884. He died in 1893 at Cuxham in Oxfordshire.

Alan Charles Thomas James 1892-1894

Alan James was a curate at Radley for about two years. He was born in about 1854 in Hindringham, Norfolk, where his father, Edward, was a vicar. In 1881 he was the curate at Walpole St Peter in Wisbech in East Anglia, lodging in the school house, and in 1891 he was at the Holy Cross Rectory in Bury, Huntingdonshire. He died on 8 June 1911.

Charles Gore 1893-1894

Charles Gore, who was born on 22 January 1853, was a notable theologian and Anglican bishop. He was the third son of the Honourable Charles Alexander Gore and brother of the fourth Earl of Arran. His mother, Augusta Lavinia Priscilla (née Ponsonby), was a daughter of the fourth Earl of Bessborough. Gore was educated at Harrow School in London before attending Balliol College, Oxford.

Charles Gore

On 25 July 1892 a group of clergy – Charles Gore, William Carter, James Nash, George Longridge, Cyril Bickersteth and Walter Howard Frere – formed the Community of the Resurrection. Their aim was to put social morality and Christian living at the forefront of the church's work. The Community of the Resurrection had rules, including that priests who were members had to be celibate and had to work in a way that would develop the faculties of other members. Worship and the service of God were paramount. Initially the group met at Pusey House, Oxford, but with Gore feeling the need to get some fresh air, a decision was made that he should accept the incumbency of Radley. He was feeling suffocated by the pressures of leading the Community and felt that Radley would give him time to obtain peace and read.

Gore had good intentions but little experience of a country parish and found it difficult to adapt his sermons to a village congregation. Nevertheless he trained the choir, formed a village band and made friends with Radley College. However, it all proved too much for him and after three months he went abroad to recuperate. On his return he was disappointed with the poor attendances in church. Good Friday turned out to be the exception as the local farmers paid their workers for the day off work if they attended church. This went against Gore's philosophy. He survived another three months at Radley before being ordered to go abroad for his health for six months. James Okey Nash (see entry below) took over the incumbency while he was away. Revd Charles Gore did not enjoy Radley as he found it an unhealthy place to live and his study was dark and dismal. There were too many people around him, which he did not like. He resigned in early 1895 and went to Westminster Abbey, where he found happiness.

Letter printed in the Radley parish magazine

MY DEAR FRIENDS   Jan 5th 1895

Nothing would have surprised me more than if anyone had told me in the autumn of last year that before Christmas I should have resigned the benefice of Radley. But I found out that, however strong I may hope to be, I could not really manage to work the parish and attend also to the other work which I have and which I cannot get rid of. So I came to feel, when I was away in the summer that I must resign. If one cannot do a bit of work, one had better give it up. After I had made this decision I was offered and accepted a Canonry at Westminster, which only made the decision more plainly necessary. And so, in fact, I resigned the benefice some fortnight or more ago. It is a great comfort to me to feel that I shall still be living with the community at the Vicarage a great part of the year. And as, I am sure, I shall be praying for the parish, so I hope I may ask your prayers for me at Westminster.

I do not think I could have persuaded myself to resign if by doing so I had brought about another complete change at the Vicarage. But, as you know very well, that my successor is to be Mr Nash, whom you all are familiar with, and, I believe trust as he deserves to be trusted. I am sure no one could have a more single desire to promote our Lord's kingdom in the parish, and your own eternal welfare. Such zeal, with the goodwill and prayers of us, must, I am sure, have God's blessing.

Let me, then, as one who is saying farewell, but not taking leave, wish you every good thing for soul and body in the coming year.

Your affectionate friend
CHARLES GORE

In his book, *The Community of the Resurrection – A Centenary History*, Alan Wilkinson wrote:

> Gore was known as a theologian, preacher, social reformer and church leader. But he was also 'an ardent fisherman, most skilful with rod and line', which cost him much in prayer, nervous effort and intellectual conflict.

Mr Sampson joined the Community in 1895, making 10 clergymen altogether in the village of Radley. Charles Gore made visits to Radley to visit the Community from time to time. The Community remained at the Vicarage until 1898 when they moved to make their headquarters at Mirfield in the West Riding of Yorkshire.

The Bishop of Zululand was a member of the Community and Charles Gore encouraged the parishioners to help him. Gore felt that the people in Radley should be doing what they could to spread the gospel among what he called the heathens. When one of the members of the Community of the Resurrection visited Charles Gore in 1896, they found him wearing green spectacles as his sight was failing him. As a result he had to give up some study and a good deal of his work, although he had recently published a book called *The Creed of the Christian*. In 1897 Gore was preaching and lecturing in Canada and the USA. While there he took part in the Convention of the Brotherhood of St Andrew.

Gore became Bishop of Worcester in 1902 and in 1905 the first Bishop of Birmingham. He was aware of the poverty and the social problems facing many of the city's citizens at the time of the new diocese and, rather than spend money on a new building, he decided to use the existing church of St Philip as the cathedral. Eight years later he retired to London. He died on 17 January 1932 and his ashes were buried at Mirfield. During his lifetime he authored or edited many books and pamphlets.

Statue to Charles Gore in the grounds of Birmingham Cathedral

Richard Belward Rackham 1893-*c*.1897

Rackham, who was born in 1863 in West Derby, Lancashire, was educated at Ely Cathedral Grammar School. Before coming to Radley as curate, he was the curate at Great Budworth in Cheshire. He wrote a book entitled *The Acts of the Apostles – An Exposition* and is described on its front page as being a member of the Community of the Resurrection. It would appear he came to Radley at the same time as Charles Gore and stayed on for a while after Gore's departure.

In 1911 Rackham was a patient in a nursing home in Upper Norwood, Surrey, though he was living at the Deanery in Wells, Somerset, at the time of his death on 27 August 1912.

James Okey Nash 1895-1898

James Nash

Nash was born in 1863 at Pernambuco in Brazil but left there to be educated in the UK. He attended King William's College on the Isle of Man before gaining an open scholarship to Hertford College in Oxford and starting his career as a curate in Bethnal Green. He was a founder of the Community of the Resurrection while at Pusey House (1880 to 1893).

When Gore left Radley, there was a delay in filling the benefice. The institution of the new incumbent, James Okey Nash, was to be on St Paul's Day, 25 January 1895, but on that date the deed of presentation had not arrived. There was, in fact, a difference between the lawyers as to whether there was to be a 'vicar' or a 'rector'. After old documents had been examined, it was decided that Nash was a 'vicar'. He was instituted by the Bishop as 'cure of souls' on 8 March 1895 and inducted to the Church and Vicarage by the vicar of Abingdon on 26 March.

Nash hoped that the villagers would support him and he hoped that they knew him well enough to know what to expect of him. He emphasised that the church, the gospel, the services and the sacraments had to be at the centre of things. He would not be satisfied if societies and amusements were to multiply without end and the worship of God to languish. The size of the congregation was a recurring theme in the parish magazine. Commenting on the Easter week services, Nash wrote in 1895 that the weekday services were well attended. He was referring to the evening services mainly, as the three daytime services were attended by the school children as it was during school time. The attendance at both Matins and Evensong on Good Friday was exceedingly good and at the 'Three Hours' service, though not so large as the others, Nash felt it was very fair for most of the time. The sermons were preached by Mr Barnes in the morning and Mr Carter in the evening. The vicar conducted the 'Three Hours' service. Many of the villagers stayed for the whole or nearly the whole time. On Easter Sunday the celebrations of the Holy Eucharist at 8am and 9am were well attended.

The vicar noted in the parish magazine that there was a plan to hold Sunday School in the afternoon, after which the children would go into the Church and be questioned on what they had learned. He hoped that the children would also attend in the morning. He discouraged children attending church in the evening unless they were sitting with their parents.

Lent services in 1896 were well attended but the vicar highlighted the problem of the villagers living a distance away from the Church, which he felt kept them away from services.

Nash used the parish magazine in 1896 as a way of communicating with his parish. His comments at times could be quite hard-hitting, especially when trying to get adults and children to attend church services. He knew how to flatter people but he also had strong opinions about certain things. He wrote about the events in school and the following is an extract from one of his articles written in November 1896:

Mrs Dockar-Drysdale is very kindly making arrangements for some lessons in cooking for the elder girls in Radley; and the girls seem eager for the opportunity, for they feel that, whether in their own home or in service, it is a great thing to be able to cook. French villagers are said to be far better than us English at making pleasant and wholesome food at small expense. And somebody once said he believed half the crime was due to bad cooking. (Is this from the husbands and big sons losing their temper and throwing things about, or because they desert their homes and get into bad ways?) But certainly, if from the same material there can come a meal which invites you to sit down and one which makes you want to go away, there is no doubt which is best. Wise housewives understand about this. It is like the difference made by a clean and comfortable, cheerful home, as against an untidy, cheerless home, in the happiness and love and temperance of that household. It is an affair first of knowing, then of thinking and taking trouble.

Writing in the parish magazine during Lent, Nash encouraged people to 'go to church more often, to give more to the church and to the collecting boxes for the heathen in Zululand'. He also wrote about the importance of fasting and that the reason for so much drunkenness, self-indulgence and laziness was because vast numbers of men let themselves 'go just as their fancy carried them'. The vicar exhorted the parishioners to abstain from alcohol. His aims were for all children to be brought up as abstainers and to have stronger men who would work better because they did not drink alcohol. He also believed that a public house was no place for a woman.

In October 1897, Nash announced in the parish magazine that the Community of the Resurrection had decided to leave Radley. The reasons he gave were that their services were needed elsewhere and they had outgrown the house (the Vicarage) now there were 11 people living there. They had come four years before with six members. This meant that Nash was also leaving Radley. He wrote that he had had his successes and failures, and had made many friends in the village. His life's ambition was to get everyone to go to church, but he did not manage this in Radley. Nor did he always get the alms he hoped for. The members of the Community finally left at the end of January 1898. Nash felt he would not forget Radley as they were going to a house owned by the mother of a former pupil at Radley College, whose chapel had a memorial window to another pupil whose home had been in Mirfield.

In the December 1897 issue of the parish magazine, Nash wrote a letter to his parishioners and announced that the Council of Radley College had offered the living to Mr Charles B. Longland who had accepted it.

After leaving Radley in 1898, Nash appears to have gone to London to see Charles Gore as he was a visitor at his house at the time of the 1901 Census. He made many visits back to Radley, mainly to preach at special services. At some point he went to South Africa and became Bishop of Cape Town. Records on the Ancestry website show him leaving Liverpool for Cape Town in 1927 and returning in 1930. He died in 1943 at the House of the Resurrection at Mirfield in Yorkshire.

Charles Boxall Longland 1898-1916

Charles Longland

Before coming to Radley, Longland, a graduate of Worcester College, Oxford, was one of the Bishop of Chester's special service clergy and was in charge of a very large parish in Tranmere, Cheshire. When he arrived in Radley he was married and had one son. His first letter in the parish magazine appeared in April 1898 where he wrote that he was trying to visit as many people as possible but found it difficult, as he was not yet living in the Vicarage.

Longland was inducted as vicar of Radley on 22 April 1898 at a ceremony performed by the vicar of Abingdon, Revd Wentworth Watson. In his address, Revd Watson explained that what the congregation had just witnessed had put the vicar in possession of his temporal rights, but that the more important part of putting him in spiritual charge of his parish had been performed privately by the Bishop of Oxford at an earlier date.

Longland was at Radley during a very busy time for the Church as it was during his incumbency that major repairs were carried out (see Chapter 2). From 1904 he combined his incumbency with that of St Swithun's Church, Kennington, but continued to live in Radley's vicarage. In 1916 he moved from Radley to become incumbent at Aston Tirrold near Wallingford in Berkshire, but continued to hold the incumbency at Kennington until 1918.

In 1886 Longland married Gertrude Martha Makins who was born in about 1862 in Surbiton. They had a son called Austin Charles who was born in 1888. In the 1901 Census she was living as head of the household in Freshwater, Isle of Wight, with her 12 year old son and maid Florence Allsop. The maid stayed with the family and was living, aged 33, with father and son in 1911 at Radley Vicarage. Also there was Constance Sarah Makins, Longland's sister-in-law who was aged 53 and single. Gertrude had died at the age of about 43 at Danesfield, Foxcombe Hill, near Oxford on 3 April 1905. Revd Richard Rackham (see entry above) of the Community of the Resurrection conducted her funeral service.

In 1925 Longland married Christiana Ellis, a spinster of Kingston-upon-Thames. His marriage certificate indicated that he was a clerk in Holy Orders at Aston Tirrold. He was 63 and she was 51.

Longland, who was born in about 1862 at Rotherfield Greys, Henley-on-Thames, died in the Acland Nursing Home in Oxford on 27 March 1940, but had been living prior to this at Clanfield House in Abingdon. Probate was given to his son Austin Charles, a barrister-at-law.

Richard Morgan Rees *c.*1905-1906

Rees is described as the curate of Radley and chaplain of Christ Church, Oxford, on several of the burial records in the Radley parish registers. Crockford's Clerical Directory of 1908 gives the dates of his curacy in Radley as above.

Charles Stanley Phillips 1916-1921

The Revd Charles Stanley Phillips succeeded Longland as vicar. He lived in the Vicarage and combined his parochial work with teaching history at Radley College. He became an assistant master of Radley College in 1917 and was rural dean of Abingdon from 1920 to 1921. On leaving Radley in 1921 he became vicar of Kings Cross, Halifax, for a year before working in Buckingham and then at Milton near Cambridge.

Phillips was a scholar at Kings College, Cambridge, graduating in 1905. He was a curate for a short time at various churches including ones in Stoke-on-Trent, Woolwich and Bury. In the 1911 Census he is recorded as single and living as a 'clergyman of the established church' at St Mary's House, Rectory House, Woolwich, London. Born about 1883 in Boston, Lincolnshire, Phillips attended Aldenham School in Hertfordshire. He died at The Homes of St Barnabas, Dormans, Surrey, on 19 November 1949.

Charles Overy 1921

Overy was born in 1882 and graduated from Christ Church, Oxford, in 1907. After working in various churches he became an assistant master at Radley College in 1919. He was there for three years before becoming vicar of St Frideswide's in Oxford. While he was at Radley College he took on the duties of priest-in-charge of the village church for the year 1921. This was the year that Charles Phillips left Radley, so presumably Overy served in the interregnum. Not much is known about Overy's subsequent career except that in 1939 he was vicar in Dursley, Gloucestershire.

The following quotes suggest that Overy was interested in both archaeology and boxing.

> From the October 1927 issue of the *Antiquaries Journal*
>
> At the end of April of last year the Revd Charles Overy drew my attention to the presence of broken animal bones, flints, and shards of pottery in a gravel-pit on the south side of the road from Abingdon to Radley, about a mile out of Abingdon.
>
> The pit lies on the very boundary of the parish of Abingdon in a field at about 200 ft. O.D., just over half a mile north of the Thames and some 30 ft. above the river. On its eastern and southern sides it is bounded by the wide trenches, which in the days of the splendour of Abingdon Abbey formed part of the Abbey's fishponds; on the north is the road, and on the east the ground drops to a little brook.
>
> From *The Radleian 1921*
>
> The debt of gratitude we already owe to the Revd Charles Overy was increased by his kindness in coming once more to act as judge and referee in the Boxing Competitions on Wednesday, March 13th. He considered that as a whole the standard was not so high as in former years, but still there is material, which may form something good in time to come.

The Ashmolean Museum in Oxford has a white flint scraper (AN1933.1720), which was presented by Revd Overy.

The Revd Charles Overy of Breakspear Cottage, Knighton, Shrivenham, died in the Acland Nursing Home, Oxford, on 1 August 1963. His widow was named as Gertrude Lovlin Overy (née O'Connell). The couple were married on 29 November 1916 in Ewell, Surrey, when he was 34 and she was 39.

Edward Heseltine Hibbert 1922-1925

Hibbert, son of a merchant, was born in 1876 in Hackney, Middlesex. He married Jessie Blackwood Blair in about 1903. The 1911 Census shows that they had three children and they were living in Beckingham Rectory, Newark. She died in about 1958 in the New Forest District. Their only son, Denys Heseltine, who was born on 17 October 1905 and died in 1977 in Stafford District, played cricket for Radley College between 1923 and 1924. Their elder daughter, Joan, was born in about 1907 and became the Director of Education for the Sudanese Government; according to *The Gazette* she received the OBE in 1954. A second daughter, Helen Angela, was born in 1910.

In 1932 Hibbert, now rector of Rockbourne, Hampshire, officiated at two weddings in June and November at Radley Church, both of which involved members of the Raworth family.

Hibbert died on 4 July 1965 at Lonsdale Nursing Home, Southsea, Hampshire. He had been living at Flat 2, Cathedral House, Portsmouth.

Thomas Hearne Liddiard 1925-1928

Thomas Liddiard was born in 1889 in Newbury, Berkshire. He married Ellen Ruth Green at St Leonard's Church, Sunningwell, in 1923 and died in 1964 in Northampton District. He is buried at Sunningwell.

Thomas Liddiard

Just before they married, Ellen's mother died leaving over £10,000 with probate being granted to Ellen, now an only child following the death of her brother during the First World War. Probate was also granted to her when her father died in 1940 leaving over £11,000. It is likely that the Liddiards lived at Bayworth Manor with Ruth's father after their marriage as this is the address given for them in Crockford's Clerical Directory of 1932. Ellen was born in 1894 and died in 1976 in Newbury District.

After studying at Corpus Christi College, Cambridge, where he gained a BA in 1913, Thomas Liddiard went to Cuddesdon College near Oxford and was ordained in 1916. Before coming to Radley he was at Summertown and Caversham. He was vicar of Kennington from 1937 to 1946 (where there is a road named after him) and then vicar of St Helen's Abingdon.

In 1946 Revd Pixell described him as a hardworking and faithful priest helped tremendously by Mrs Liddiard. For many years there was a brass plaque to Thomas Hearne Liddiard on the main gate at Radley Church commemorating his time at Radley and his appointment as an honorary canon of Christ Church, Oxford.

Arthur Aubert Jackson 1929-1936

Arthur Jackson was born in about 1864 in Wormley, Hertfordshire, and attended Charterhouse School in Godalming, Surrey. From 1891 to 1892 he was a curate at South Hinksey and then became vicar of Horspath. In 1911 he was in Ashurst, Sussex. By then he was aged 46 and his wife, Eva Frances Ray (formerly Styles) was 34. They were married on 1 October 1895 in Swanscombe, Kent. They had three children, Phillip Arthur born about 1908, Eva born about 1897 and Robert born about 1900. Eva Katherine Mary Jackson of Radley married Dennis Anderton Brigg (a medical practitioner) at Radley Church on 16 Oct 1930.

Arthur Jackson

Revd Jackson was sometime rector of Ashurst in Sussex and Little Hallingbury in Essex, and Chaplain of Magdalen College, Oxford. He died suddenly on 3 July 1946 aged 82 after being an invalid for several years.

Francis Daly Briscoe 1936-1939

Francis Briscoe was born in 1877 in Great Heaton, Lancashire, the son of Peter and Mary Alice Briscoe. During the First World War, he was a chaplain in the New Zealand Chaplains Department and was attached to the New Zealand Expeditionary Force. He returned on the *Corinthia* to England on 31 December 1920, aged 43, from Wellington, New Zealand, to the House of the Divine Compassion in Plaistow, London. Briscoe died on 8 November 1960 at Redhill County Hospital, Surrey. He had been living at The Homes of St Barnabas, Dormans, Surrey.

Francis Briscoe

While at Radley, Briscoe occupied only the old part of the Vicarage. The part added during the time of Warden Wood (see Chapter 2) was now being used to house an overflow of eight boys from Radley College.

Eustace Edward Arthur Heriz-Smith 1939-1941

Heriz-Smith was born on 15 November 1887 in Jersey, Channel Islands. He married Frances Joan Ewer on 21 December 1911. They had two children: Eustace Peter (born 1916), who served in the Kenyan police force, and Patrick Ambrose Lewis (1920-2011), who became an art teacher and artist.

Eustace Heriz-Smith

Heriz-Smith studied at Pembroke College, Cambridge, before becoming a schoolmaster at Sherborne School. *The Gazette* of 11 September 1918 announced his appointment as a temporary chaplain to the Forces.

While at Radley, Heriz-Smith wrote *The Sinner and the Cross. Meditations for Good Friday. On the Words from the Cross.* He died in 1983 aged 95 in Bath. His wife had died in 1961 aged about 74.

John Vincent Pixell 1941-1957

John Pixell

In 1955 S.P.B. Mais, a reporter with the *Oxford Mail* wrote an article about Radley. He described the vicar, Revd Pixell, as someone who had 'thrown himself heart and soul into the none-too-easy work of coping with a large and scattered parish composed of very diversified social and economic strata of society'. Mais commented on the fact that the vicar did not let the handicap of a leg twice broken deter him from visiting his parishioners in and out of season. He knew the life history of them all. The vicar was also complimented on the fact that he managed to live on his own in a vicarage that was about eight times too big for him and that he was able, in his leisure time, to build with his own hands garages and outbuildings. Pixell, Mais said, was known as a man who spoke his own mind and after 14 years' service he was treated with respect by the parishioners.

The above was endorsed by current Radley resident, Jenny Davie, who wrote:

> Reading from Pam's 'From the Vicar' page of last month's *Radley News*, which recalls the Revd Pixell (vicar from 1941 to 1957) brought back many memories.

> He had close ties to Radley Primary School and lots of activities centred on the church services, brass rubbings, nature studies in the old church yard, which was always full of wild flowers and we were taught all their names. This was prior to it being tidied up!

> We all went to Sunday School on Sunday afternoons and were very proud of the sticker we received each time we attended which we stuck in our attendance books. Both Miss Cross as Headmistress of the village school and Revd Pixell also encouraged children to become choir members and bell ringers. My moment of fame, along with Janet Steptoe, was a picture in the *Girl* magazine showing us as the youngest bell ringers. We were both standing on orange boxes in order to reach the ropes.

> Prior to coming to Radley, the Revd Pixell served in the East End of London and set up Youth Clubs for boys. Other memories were his very thick lens glasses, which were probably the cause of his notoriously bad driving.

> Mrs Pearman was his housekeeper for many years.

> I think he played an important part in our formative years and I remember him fondly.

Pixell was baptised in Frampton Cotterell, Gloucestershire, in 1882. He married Melvina L. Fox in 1941 in Poplar, London. She was born in 1883 in Reigate, the daughter of Edward Fox, a metal broker. Their marriage was relatively short lived as Melvina died in December 1943.

Revd Pixell went into the village school on Friday morning each week. In May 1943, some of the older children cycled to Woodstock after the service for Ascension Day with the Revd Pixell, who was probably aged over 60 at this time, and Miss Cross.

In January 1945, the vicar appeared to be living at The Lodge, Radley College, as that was the address he gave when writing in *Radley News*. Eastbourne College had been evacuated to Radley College during the war and it is possible that the Vicarage, especially the newer part, was being used for the extra students and staff. It would probably have been more comfortable for the widowed Revd Pixell at The Lodge. In July 1945 he wrote:

> We shall be saying goodbye to Eastbourne College at the end of this term as they are returning to Eastbourne. I know they will be glad to get back to their own buildings.

During the fuel crisis in the very cold winter of 1946-47, it was impossible to buy any coke for the stove in the Church. So Revd Pixell suggested that parishioners should bring a hot water bottle with them and put on extra clothing if they wanted to face the rigours of an unheated church.

At Christmas in 1953, there was what could have been a disastrous arson attack on the Church. The Revd Pixell was at Sunningwell Church with Radley schoolboys Brian Ford, Bruce Gaskell, David Herridge and Peter King when the news of the fire reached him. There followed a hair-raising dash by car to Radley by the vicar, who was not known for his careful driving. The boys accompanying him were terrified.

In January 1947 Pixell wrote about another experience he had with his car.

> There is nothing like being in trouble to find out the value of kindness of other people! I was caught out in Oxford during one foggy Tuesday evening and had to get back home with the car. As far as the Railway Bridge the going was not too bad but then I ran into a bad patch in Kennington and ended up in a hedge which saved me from going down a bank into a waste piece of land and turning over. Mr Shirley (New Road) was following me in his car and he stopped to help and several others from Kennington came to lend a hand and eventually after lifting the back of the car on to solid ground another car pulled me once again on to the roadway. Mr Shirley then led me back to safety.

Pixell died on 21 September 1965 in Abingdon Hospital. He was then living at 247 Radley Road, Abingdon.

Robert Springett Brutton 1957-1965

Linda Thomas, who was a pupil at Radley Primary School from 1957 to 1963, remembers the Revd Brutton. He went into school once a week and often used to walk home with the children and visit their families. He was a popular vicar who tried to welcome everyone to the village and encourage them to take part in village activities.

Brutton was born on 30 May 1914 in Lustleigh, Devon. He married Elizabeth Phayre Irwin in 1944 and had three children, Susan, Judy and Timothy.

Robert Brutton with his wife

In July 1939, when Brutton received his Royal Aero Flying Club's flying certificate, his occupation was given as a 'brewer' as he was a member of the family brewing business in Yeovil, Somerset. He studied history and law at Trinity College, Cambridge, before returning to the business.

Robert met his wife in Paris in a taxi when they were returning from separate trips abroad. Soon after their engagement, however, the Second World War separated them. Robert was posted to Burma and India, and Elizabeth started work for MI5 in England. Later she managed to get a posting to India and they were married in Bombay Cathedral in 1944.

After the war, the Bruttons went to live in Somerset where Robert was responsible for looking after the landlords and buildings of the family's public houses. It was a surprise to everyone when he left to join the church in 1954. He trained at Cuddesdon College, Oxford, before becoming curate at Wendover, near Aylesbury, and then vicar at Radley. He had extraordinary people skills and put them to good effect when dealing with people, whether they were churchgoers or not. The congregation at Radley increased.

When he left Radley in 1965 he went to Sonning-on-Thames in Berkshire. Below is an extract from his obituary in the Sonning parish magazine.

> His gift of listening, caring, and genuinely showing an interest in everyone he met meant he became a much loved figure and the novel approach he adopted in his ministries ensured that his church services were always full! His second ministry, nine years later, was here at Sonning where he established himself again as a firm favourite, filling the church with young and old alike. His trademark was a short sermon, usually no longer than 5-10 minutes. Years later people still comment on how powerful his sermons were and how they can still recall the wonderfully clear message that he was able to put across. He frequently used various props to demonstrate and drive a point home. He was always out and about in the village helping to cut someone's hedge or visiting the Scout or Brownie meeting.

> He was an extraordinary person who was an example to us all with his unfailing kindness, patience, tolerance, supportiveness and huge capacity to see the best in everyone. Truly a great man who has left a legacy of love.

> Following retirement in 1973 Robert and Elizabeth moved to the Isle of Purbeck where he enjoyed gardening, sailing, visits from his children and grandchildren and also taking a few church services.

> Revd Robert Springett Brutton died at home on Easter Saturday, 15 April 2006, aged 91. A Service of Thanksgiving was held at St Andrews Church, Sonning-on-Thames on

Friday 28 April at 2.30 pm. Donations in lieu of flowers were given to the Alzheimer's Society. His wife had died four years previously. Their ashes are interred in Sonning churchyard, overlooking the small stained glass window restored to mark his incumbency.

Sydney Ernest Allso 1966-1971

Sydney Allso was born on 28 March 1910 in Birmingham. His parents were Ernest, a clerk, and Emily (née Chaplin). In 1937 he was living at the vicarage in Stroud Green, Hornsey and in December 1940 he enlisted as a Royal Army Chaplain. He married Winifred Stone in 1944 in Lincoln District. In 1950, Allso accepted the benefice of Tattershall and went to East Finchley in 1953. It was while at the latter benefice that he wrote the following letter to *The Times*.

Sydney Allso

Letter to *The Times*, May 1954

Sir,

I am sure that all Cornishmen would be grateful if they could depend on *The Times* to keep alive the ancient and only correct name for the Helston festival of May 8 – the Furry Dance derived from the Cornish for festival. A pamphlet published by the Helston Old Cornwall Society in 1931 suggests that the substitution of Flora for Furry was simply a piece of eighteenth century classicism which imagined a connexion between the ancient Furry Day festival and that of the Roman goddess Flora. May 8 is of course the spring festival of St Michael the Archangel, who appears in the ancient seals of the borough as the patron saint of the town.

I am, Sir, your obedient servant,

Sydney E Allso

All Saints Vicarage, Twyford Avenue, N2

Sidney Allso wrote to *The Times* in November 1967 while he was at Radley. This was in response to the Bishop of Stafford who had suggested that, instead of creating new dioceses to ease the workload of some of the clergy, they should combine the five Episcopal areas into one diocese. The bishops would remain but work as a team. This would not add any extra cost to the church as the first plan had indicated.

Diocesan Boundaries. Letter to the Editor.

Sir, Heaven forbid that I should be governed by a board of bishops – which it seems to me is what the Bishop of Stafford's proposal (your report November 7) would mean.

Surely the whole point of episcopacy is that we should be able to look to *one* bishop as our father-in-God, and that his diocesan family should be of a size that enables him to fulfil this function.

Why is it assumed that the creation of more dioceses must necessarily involve the Church in vastly increased expenditure? In a small diocese the Bishop's expenses would be less (and also he would probably be able to manage with a smaller stipend), and the office of archdeacon would become superfluous. Although the Diocesan would need to have the use of a church as his cathedral, I see no reason at all for creating new residentiary-canonries.

If we could go one step further and bring into being more provinces, then most of the work, which at present is dealt with by the various diocesan boards and committees could be done on a provincial basis.

Yours faithfully,

Sydney E Allso,

Radley Vicarage, Abingdon Berkshire.

Winifred Allso started the very successful Women's Fellowship in Radley. At that time there was a Mothers' Union and a Young Wives club. As there were restrictions on membership of the former and the latter were getting older, Mrs Allso thought that it would be better to combine the two and call the group the 'Women's Fellowship'.

Allso's book, *Radley Church and Parish,* was published in 1971, the year he left Radley. In 1976 Sydney and his wife were living at The Vicarage, Skegby Road, Annesley Woodhouse, Mansfield. He died on 26 December 1992 and was buried at Holy Trinity Churchyard, Tattershall, East Lindsey, Lincolnshire. Winifred died on 3 October 1979.

Following Allso's departure from Radley, there was a short period without a vicar. Services and other parish activities were maintained by Radley College's Chaplain (Revd J.M. Jenkins) and Assistant Chaplain (Revd D.S. Coulton), together with R.W. Stoughton-Harris, one of the assistant masters.

Daniel Legh Pope 1971-1988

Dan Pope came late to the ministry having had other occupations. On leaving school he joined the Merchant Navy; records on Ancestry show that he was on board the *Empire Waterhen* in 1942, having sailed from Newport, Monmouthshire, via Belfast to New York. He was aged 18 and was a third radio operator. By the time he was on his way to join the *Northern Master* in 1945 in Westwego, New Orleans, he was described as a first radio operator. During the Second World War Dan served for two years with the Royal Australian Navy.

Dan Pope

Dan married Josephine Morfa James in 1946. She had joined the WRNS after leaving school and worked on secret duties at Bletchley Park. Following their marriage Dan and Morfa farmed together for 10 years until Dan joined the Milk Marketing Board as a senior executive, raising a family of three children during this time. They went to live in Merrow, near Guildford, but Dan was being drawn towards his calling as a priest and he went for training at Cuddesdon College, near Oxford.

Following his ordination he took a curacy in Llanelli, the largest parish in Wales at that time, and in 1971 he successfully applied to fill the vacancy at Radley. Many of his parishioners from Llanelli attended his induction service at Radley. While he had been in Llanelli he had been actively involved with the NSPCC, the Old People's Welfare Committee and the Burma Star Association. So began 18 happy years in Radley, although in 1977 he suffered a life-threatening illness from which thankfully he made a full recovery. He was a very popular vicar who tried to get to know all his parishioners and welcomed Christians of all denominations to worship in the only church in Radley.

Dan was born in Wales on 26 September 1923 and like a lot of Welsh people he loved music and language. He had an annual engagement to preach in Welsh at Jesus College, Oxford, but did not have many opportunities to use the Welsh language in Radley.

In 1987 Dan was invited to take over the Anglican chaplaincy of Kyrenia in northern Cyprus. It was not an easy decision for him, but he accepted. He made a success of it and built up a good relationship with both the ex-pats and local Turkish Cypriots. He was there until 1990.

Dan and Morfa came back to England in 1990 and he spent his last years in Shipley in Sussex. After Dan's death in 2000, Morfa came back to live in Radley where she died in 2007.

Walter John (Jock) Fletcher-Campbell, 1977 and 1989

Jock, as he was known to everyone, was born in Hampshire in 1912. After studying at Radley College and then Magdalen College, Oxford, where he rowed in the early 1930s in the very successful college eight, he took Holy Orders in 1938. In 1935, Jock visited Lagos (Nigeria), leaving on the *Usaramo* on 17 January and returning on the *Tanganyika* on 21 April. The passenger lists record his age as 23 and his home address as Paddock Cottage, Lymington, Hampshire.

Jock had a long and interesting career, as shown by the list below of the incumbencies he held:

- curate of St Mary's, Portsmouth (wartime);
- vicar of Sarisbury in Hampshire, 1945;
- vicar of St James, Portsmouth, 1947 to 1960;
- rural dean of Portsmouth, 1955 to 1960;
- Metropolitan Secretary, Society for the Propagation of the Gospel 1960 and its Deputy Home Secretary from 1967 to 1970;
- vicar of Stanton Harcourt with Northmoor, 1970 to 1975;
- priest-in-charge of Bampton, Clanfield, Lew, Aston and Shifford, 1975 to 1976;
- rural dean of Witney from 1971 to 1976;
- rural dean of Abingdon from 1980 to 1987.

In 1977 Jock took charge of the parish of Radley for almost a year while Dan Pope was ill. He also took many of the services after Dan Pope had left and before Keith Kinnaird arrived.

In 1989 Jock acted as an assistant honorary curate to help Father Keith, who was not able to move into the Vicarage with his wife until the following year (see entry below). Jock continued to support Radley Church in various ways including, on occasions, carrying out the practical task of cutting the grass in the churchyard.

'Jock' Fletcher Campbell

Jock's son, Christopher, taught at Radley College from 1972 to 1980, and there was at least a term when he was joined by his father who came to teach divinity. Jock died on 27 November 2008, having been living in Upper Road, Kennington. His wife, known as 'Bettie', survived him along with their son Christopher and daughter Felicity. Jock maintained his interest in rowing and, at the time of his death, was the oldest and longest-serving member of the Leander Club.

Keith Kinnaird 1988-1995

Keith Kinnaird began his working life as an accountant. Although the first stirrings of a call to the priesthood came when he was just 17, it was not until some 10 years later that he finally decided to seek ordination. After training at Chichester Theological College Father Keith, as he was commonly addressed, was ordained in 1975 and appointed curate of St Peter's Church, Didcot, where he was involved in the building of a new church in the centre of the parish. Next he was appointed to the parish of Abingdon where he was priest-in-charge of St Michael & All Angels and chaplain of Abingdon Hospital. Other duties included acting as chaplain to the Society of St Margaret community of nuns at their convent in Marcham Road and working with various schools in the town.

Keith Kinnaird

In 1982 the Bishop of Oxford appointed Father Keith to be the next parish priest of Sunningwell with the intention that it would unite with another parish, possibly Wootton, as a result of pastoral reorganisation within the Abingdon Deanery. In the event a different pattern ensued. When Dan Pope left Radley in 1988, Radley College, as patron, advertised the vacancy, which attracted over 70 applicants. However, the College's choice was not acceptable to the Oxford Diocese because its scheme for pastoral reorganisation was to unite Sunningwell and Radley (see Chapter 1). Father Keith was summoned by the Bishop of Oxford, who had been in consultation with Radley College, and told 'I wish you to be father of a larger family'. So, on 8 November 1988, the warden of Radley College, Dennis Silk, presented Father Keith to the Rt Revd Graham Foley, Bishop of Reading (Radley was then in the Archdeaconry of Berkshire) at a special service of inauguration in Radley Church as the new parish priest.

Father Keith was now responsible for the pastoral care of two parishes with identical times of services and two Church of England primary schools on whose governing bodies he sat. Much effort was given to the interaction between the two parishes, not least in having to spread the times of services to enable the vicar to minister effectively. In the early days he had some help from Revd Jock Fletcher-Campbell as honorary assistant curate. Later on, a lay pastoral team of readers and ministers (see Chapter 7) was created with the Bishop's approval to assist Father Keith in ministering to the benefice.

There was a delay before the Kinnairds could move to Radley because the Vicarage was uninhabitable pending alterations to extend the old part and detach the Victorian Gore House (see Chapter 2). Following a special service of Evensong on 25 March 1990 attended by the Rt Revd John Bone, Bishop of Reading, there was a procession to the newly restored Vicarage for a re-dedication and blessing.

In 1992, Father Keith hosted a teaching mission to mark the centenary of Charles Gore's ministry. Distinguished speakers included former Bishops of Oxford and brethren from the Community of the Resurrection in which Father Keith became a companion.

In 1995 Father Keith was invited by the Bishop of Chichester to move to West Sussex to be vicar of the new Benefice of Old Shoreham and New Shoreham. In 2000 he was invited back to the Diocese of Oxford to take up the living of St Andrew's, Caversham Heights, Berkshire. After his retirement in 2007, the Kinnairds moved to Wantage.

Father Keith had a very varied ministry, including being the Bishop's Adviser for Vocations to the Sacred Ministry and Ministry of Deliverance and Healing. In 1991 he was invested to a serving brother to the Most Venerable Order of the Hospital of St John of Jerusalem and was chaplain at Abingdon Hospital between 1975 and 1995. Father Keith's wife, Pam, was very supportive in his ministry and was secretary at Radley Primary School while they lived in Radley.

Thomas Patrick Gibbons 1996-2004

Tom Gibbons came to the benefice of Radley and Sunningwell with his wife and young family from north-east England, where he had been working in an urban team ministry. The family lived in Radley Vicarage.

During his period at Radley, Tom featured in both the local and national press. In 2002, Greene King, the owners of the Bowyer Arms, stopped showing *Sky Sports* in the pub on the grounds that '*Sky* was not profitable'. An article in the *Oxford Mail* at the time described how the regulars, led by the vicar, a keen Newcastle United and rugby union supporter, had started a petition to get it reinstated. Later the same year, Tom was

Tom Gibbons

interviewed by the late Cassandra Jardine for an article in the *Daily Telegraph*. Jardine cites him as an example of one of the church's characters 'too independent to knuckle down to the nine-to-seven world of city life' and found it hard to 'imagine him during his spell as an accountant'. Tom admitted to Jardine that he supposed he was 'a bit of a maverick'. He had a fascination for 2CV cars and had quite a collection on the Vicarage drive at one time; one of the cars was painted black and white in the colours of Newcastle United. He told Jardine he had taught himself car mechanics because he was 'unable to afford £40 garage bills'. Tom also had a talent for writing poetry.

While Tom was at Radley, the Upper Cemetery (see Chapter 4) was consecrated and an open church scheme was introduced whereby the Church was kept unlocked during the week for visitors. Tom also served as chair of the governors of Radley Primary School.

Tom left Radley to go to a parish in Buckinghamshire. He is now back in the north-east working as a hospital chaplain for the County Durham and Darlington NHS Foundation Trust.

Pamela Joyce (Pam) McKellen 2004 to October 2016

Pam came to the joint benefice of Radley and Sunningwell in 2004. In 2015, the parish of Kennington also became vacant and Pam was asked to take on the new benefice of Radley, Sunningwell and Kennington. She is the first female vicar of these parishes and the third incumbent in a row at Radley to have had a different profession before becoming a priest. Pam is assisted in the benefice by Revd Glynis Beckett (Associate Minister), Revd Alison Mathew (Associate Minister) and Revd Tony Rogerson (retired minister).

Pam McKellen

Born in Sale, Cheshire, Pam's first job was teaching maths at a comprehensive school in Manchester. After five years of teaching Pam was invited to move to London to become assistant director of Crusaders, a Christian youth organisation where her role included organising a large holiday programme, leadership training, and working on national bodies on such issues as safety and child protection. After moving to a similar organisation, Pam did some consultancy work in management and fundraising, particularly in schools in the UK and Ireland. Eventually, after it had been suggested by a number of people, she was selected to train for the ministry. This involved a move to Durham. Her first role was as a curate at St Matthew's Church in Oxford.

Pam served as Area Dean of the Abingdon Deanery for five years, a job which involved strategic thinking with the Bishop, Archdeacon and other Area Deans and having an overview of the other churches in the deanery. Working with other clergy colleagues and churches was fun and led to all sorts of extra opportunities. It also included helping fill staff vacancies and welcoming new clergy to the deanery.

At other times, Pam was involved in diocesan initiatives, taking part in a variety of things including fundraising, the training of curates, and a committee looking at links with dioceses in other parts of the world. She was also a governor of a bible college.

Being vicar of Radley, Sunningwell and Kennington is a busy and varied job. A lot of planning and effort goes into coordinating the work of the three churches. Baptisms, funerals and marriages present all sorts of opportunities to meet people at times of great joy and sadness, but the church supports people at all stages of life. There are many meetings to attend, planning to do, work as a school governor, and liaison with other bodies and the Diocese. There have been challenges too, especially when Radley Church was faced in 2008 with damage caused by death watch beetle and in 2015 with the need for urgent repairs to the bells (see Chapter 2).

Pam enjoys living in Radley Vicarage. She says it is a privilege to live in a house that has been inhabited by a person of God since the middle ages. Until the beginning of the twenty-first century, women could not be ordained and there are some people who still struggle with this issue but Pam respects their views. Half of the clergy in the Church of England are now women. In May 2016 Pam announced her intention to retire in October 2016.

Kevin Wright 2010-2013

Kevin Wright

Kevin was born in Gloucester into a committed Christian family. After studying chemistry at Southampton University, Kevin became a science teacher and taught in various schools for over 30 years. Kevin offered himself for ordination when he was 54 and was accepted onto the Oxford Ministry Course at Cuddesdon College. He was ordained a deacon[2] in 2010 and priest a year later. During his work as a curate in training at Radley, Sunningwell and Kennington where he 'learned the ropes' of what being a vicar involves, Kevin worked particularly with the men of the parish, but also helped with music, all-age worship and Messy Church.

Kevin married Chris in 1973 and they have two daughters and two grandsons. He is now rector of three Somerset villages, Woolavington with Cossington and Bawdrip.

Anthony (Tony) Rogerson 1998 to the present day

Tony was born in Middlesex but the family moved soon afterwards to Harpenden where he attended St Alban's School. During his time at Trinity College, Oxford, where he read history, Tony joined the University Air Squadron as well as partaking in many sports including rowing. It was while he was in Oxford that Tony met and later married Heather. His national service was in the RAF, but his short-sightedness stopped him from flying and so he became an education officer in Shropshire, where the eldest of his three sons was born.

---

[2] After training, clergy spend an 'apprentice' year as a deacon, carrying out many but not all of the functions of a priest before being ordained to that role.

Tony came from a church-going family (both grandfathers were vicars) but for many years the church meant nothing to him. However, soon after his marriage he became a committed Christian and was accepted for ordination, but with a wife and young family, he decided the time was not quite right. Instead he joined the Atomic Energy Authority for two years before rejoining the RAF where his first position was as an education officer at the V bomber station at Honington in Suffolk. Teaching liberal studies at the RAF Engineering College, Henlow, was followed by the post of head of English at RAF College, Cranwell. Tony then transferred to the US Air Force Academy in Colorado where he taught political science. While there the family enjoyed exploring the country in their VW camper. He also came into contact at this time with a Christian organisation called the Navigators which would play a part later in his life. After a few years, however, the RAF wanted him back and Tony became head of instructional techniques at RAF Newton.

Tony Rogerson

After 16 years in the RAF, Tony left to join the staff of Navigators. He bought a house in Wimbledon and began training Christian leaders in churches and on university campuses. This took him round the world and often to Nigeria. A further change in direction came when he and Heather joined two friends in starting up a management training company, Cygnet Business Development. In 2001 Tony left this company and set up his own small company helping people to think about what they want to do next in life. There was far less pressure and he was able to devote more time to the church.

In 1966 Tony became a lay reader (see Chapter 7) and served in that capacity for many years in both the RAF and local churches. Tony and Heather moved to Radley in 1990 and he became a licensed lay minister at Radley in October 1991. However, he increasingly felt he was being called to the ordained ministry. Following study at the St Albans and Oxford Ministry Course at St Stephen's College, Oxford, Tony was ordained as a deacon in 1998 and as a priest in 1999, becoming a non-stipendiary minister serving Radley and Sunningwell. Tony is now officially retired but is still allowed to officiate and continues to serve in all three churches in the benefice. October 2016 marks his 50th year of service as reader/priest and his 25th year serving Radley Church.

Glynis Beckett 2010 to the present day

Glynis has been a member of the congregation in Sunningwell for a number of years and was Keith Kinnaird's pastoral assistant. She was ordained in 2010 and is now an Associate Minister. Part of her work has been with international students at Lady Margaret Hall, Oxford. After retiring from paid work she is looking forward to being able to spend a bit more time helping in the churches. Glynis enjoys baptisms, weddings and funerals although she likes being a part of the Iona team too.

Alison Mathew 2015 to the present day

Alison was licensed to join the team in Radley, Sunningwell and Kennington in September 2015. She works part-time in the benefice and lives in Kennington Vicarage. She wrote the following about herself for the October 2015 edition of *Radley News*:

> I am really looking forward to starting as your Associate Minister. I grew up in Dunoon on the west coast of Scotland, then started my working life as a nurse, mainly in the community. I then moved to public health and on to Tearfund Christian Development charity. Whilst there, I did a degree in English and creative writing. Gradually I felt called to become more involved in ministry and worked as an administrator in our parish church before starting my training at Ripon College, Cuddesdon. I served my curacy at St Mary's, Osterley.
>
> My husband Malcolm is a consultant anaesthetist in London. He is a medical reservist and has served overseas with the army and RAF. We have a friendly golden retriever named Bramble and, in between walks, I enjoy going to the theatre, creative writing, baking and watching re-runs of the *West Wing*!

Sources

Books

A Biographical Dictionary of the Living Authors of Great Britain and Ireland, 1814

A Classical Dictionary, John Lemprière, 1788

A History of Abingdon, J. Townsend, 1910

A Memoir of the Reverend George Wharton, Precentor of St Peter's College, Radley, Roscoe Beddoes, 1931

Cambridge University Alumni 1261–1900, compiled by John Venn and John Archibald Venn

John Lemprière (c.1765–1824), Richard Smail, 2004

London 1808-1870: The Infernal Wen, Francis Sheppard, 1971

No Ordinary Place, Radley College and the Public School System 1847–1997, Christopher Hibbert, 1997

Radley Church and Parish, Sydney E. Allso, 1971

Radley Farms and Families 1600–2011, Christine Wootton, 2011

Radley. Ancient Barrows to Modern Parish, Patrick Drysdale, 1985

St Paul's: The Cathedral Church of London 604–2004, Derek Keene, Arthur Burns and Andrew Sait (eds), 2004

St Swithun's Church Kennington, Stanley Gillam, 1994

The Church and Parish of St Nicolas, Abingdon, and other Papers, Arthur E. Preston, 1929

The Community of the Resurrection – A Centenary History, Alan Wilkinson, 1992

The Diocese Books of Samuel Wilberforce, edited by Ronald and Margaret Pugh, Oxfordshire Record Society, Volume 66, 2008

The History and Antiquities of the University of Oxford, Anthony Wood, 1796

The History of Merchant Taylors' School, from its Foundation to the Present Time, Harry Bristow Wilson, 1814

The History of Radley School, Christine Wootton, 2008

The Life of Anthony à Wood from the year 1632 to 1672, Anthony à Wood and Thomas Hearne, 1772

The Lives of Those Eminent Antiquaries John Leland, Thomas Hearne, and Anthony Wood, edited by William Huddesford, 1732-1772

The Martlet and the Griffen – An Illustrated History of Abingdon School, Thomas Hinde and Michael St John Parker, 1997

Websites

Abingdon Area Archaeological and Historical Society, www.abingdon.gov.uk/history/people/john-pendarves

Ancestry, www.ancestry.co.uk

British History Online: Alumni Oxonienses 1500-1714, www.british-history.ac.uk/alumni-oxon/1500-1714

Clergy of the Church of England Database, http://theclergydatabase.org.uk

Findmypast, www.findmypast.co.uk

Oxfordshire Library service: www.oxfordshire.gov.uk/cms/public-site/reference-online

Radley Church, http://stjamesthegreatradley.org

Documents

Document headed 'Vicars' found among the diocesan records in the Berkshire Record Office (BRO) listing Radley vicars and other information from 1610 to 1808

Biographical notes on four Radley College wardens who were also vicars of Radley, Oxford University Alumni 1500 to 1886, A.C. Money

Parliamentary papers. House of Commons and Command. Vol 1; Vol 9. Great Britain, Parliament, House of Commons

Radley Parish Records: Registers of Baptisms (1599-1950), Marriages (1599-1961) and Burials (1599-1980) transcribed by Oxfordshire Family History Society

The Thompson Family: A Search into History, Edward Thompson, www.mikesclark.com/genealogy/portraits/Thompson_Family.pdf

Thurlow, E., 'A Neolithic Site at Abingdon, Berks', *The Antiquaries Journal*, Vol. 7, No. 4, pp. 438-464.

Directories

Crockford's Clerical Directories

Kelly's Directories

Vale of White Horse directories

Other sources

Amanda Ingram, archivist at Pembroke College, Oxford

Jackson's Oxford Journal

Oxford Dictionary of National Biography

Radley History Club archives

Radley History Club's 'A Tale to Tell' recordings of interviews with local people

Radley History Club transcripts of will documents

Photographs courtesy Joyce Huddleston, Keith Kinnaird, Pam McKellen, Ann Purbrick, Christine Wootton and Radley History Club archives

Chapter 6: Tithes, Accounts and Charitable Giving

by Richard Dudding

Like any other organisation, Radley Church has throughout its existence had expenditure commitments: the incumbent vicar has had to be remunerated; the fabric of the building has had to be maintained; and it has had a role in helping the poor locally and in promoting wider charitable causes. The Church has also received charitable donations, both for its own essential purposes and in trust for providing for others.

Over the centuries the nature of this spending has changed, as have the sources of income, in ways which reflect wider social and institutional changes. The records are patchy, with some frustrating gaps. Much of potential interest is simply not known. But where records do exist, they are often very detailed, providing insights into the times of much wider relevance than the purely financial.[1]

This chapter looks at these issues from several different angles:

- tithes and the remuneration of incumbents;
- bequests in wills and other gifts;
- churchwardens' accounts;
- gifts and fundraising;
- helping the poor of the village;
- wider charitable causes.

These categorisations to some extent reflect the nature of the evidence sources. The division between them is not neat and tidy, but they enable some of the main points of interest to be drawn out.

Tithes and the remuneration of incumbents

Readers of Trollope's *Chronicles of Barsetshire* will know that in the nineteenth century the remuneration of clergy varied greatly between parishes and did so in ways which bore little or no relationship to the extent of the duties falling on the incumbent. The differences had their origins some centuries back.

In medieval times, clergy were financed locally from the product of the land. Depending on circumstance a parish church might have its own glebe land, from which it would derive the full income. More significantly the system of tithes meant that the church received a tenth of the product of other people's land. Each church normally had a rector who received the 'great tithes' and a vicar who received the 'little tithes', sometimes known as 'tithes white'. Custom varied but the great tithes were normally the direct product of the land (such as grain crops and hay) and little tithes the indirect product and/or minor products (such as lambs, pigs,

---

[1] Cash amounts quoted are in prices at the time. To provide some comparison, an agricultural labourer might have earned 7d a day in 1600, 10d in 1700, 19d in 1800 and 30d in 1900.

eggs, cheese and nuts). The rights to rectoral tithes were often held by monasteries and, after dissolution, these were acquired by lay people who might have no interest in the church other than the ownership of the income stream.

Tithes were traditionally paid in kind but over time were increasingly paid as equivalent cash sums. The Tithe Commutation Act 1836 provided for all remaining tithes in kind to be paid as cash. This commutation exercise required major surveys of landholdings, accompanied by detailed maps, which provide a rich source of local records. The clergy of Trollope's time would have been receiving cash amounts following this commutation exercise.

What then of Radley? We know the early arrangements for tithes in some detail as they are set out in a document of 1271 under which the vicar of St Helen's Abingdon was appointed. At this time Radley was a chapel within his parish and the document required him to appoint a chaplain. It provided as follows in respect of tithes:

> The same vicar [of St Helen's] will also have oblations and all other tithes pertaining to the alterage of the chapels of Radley, Drayton, Shippon and Sandford, except the tithes of lambs, wool and cheese, all of which the said abbot and convent [of Abingdon] have in the above-mentioned chapels; if however there are not enough lambs for tithe, but money is given instead, the official assigns that to the vicar's portion, likewise where a parishioner cannot conveniently make cheese owing to the shortage of animals and renders money instead … The said abbot and convent will receive all tithes of sheaves in both fields and gardens and all tithes of hay pertaining to St Helen's and its chapels … Further they will have all ... tithes of lambs, wool and cheese from Radley, Drayton, Shippon and Sandford …

Thus the Abbey and Convent of Abingdon was the rector of the parish of St Helen's and received the larger tithes.[2] The vicar of St Helen's received the smaller tithes. Radley, with the status of a chaplaincy, received nothing though the vicar of St Helen's would have had to remunerate the chaplain. No mention is made of any glebe land in Radley. We know from manorial surveys of 1547 and 1633, and a church terrier of 1678, that glebe land was not significant in Radley.[3]

The 1678 terrier lists tithes 'belonging to the Vicar of Radley' as follows:

> Item: all tithes of apples, nuts, eggs, hemp, pigs and cows

This wording tells us that the tithes were by now paid to the vicar of Radley (as he now was), rather than to the vicar of St Helen's. It is not possible to put a precise date on this significant change, but it is likely to have happened after the Stonhouses acquired the Manor of Radley in 1560 (see Chapter 1). The wording of Sir William Stonhouse's will of 1631/2, quoted later in this chapter, suggests that it had taken place by then.

---

[2] The arrangements gave the Abbey and Convent a larger share of the tithes than was typical. They included tithes of wool, sheep and cheese which would have more typically gone to the vicar.

[3] A small parcel of glebe land does, however, still exist to the north of the Vicarage.

We do not have a further account of Radley's tithes until the tithe commutation award of 1849. The assessor found that the vicar of Radley was the owner of:

> ... all manner of small tithes arising and renewing on the titheable lands of the said parish excepting only the tithe of lambs when the number is ten or any multiple of ten and except the tithe of wool when the fleeces are ten or any multiple of ten and except the tithe of milk when enough is yielded to make ten cheeses or any multiple of ten.

The assessor ruled that these tithes should be converted into a cash sum of £70 a year. He also allocated cash sums as follows to three other tithe owners, who almost certainly had inherited rectoral tithes originally owned by Abingdon Abbey and Convent before the dissolution.

Henry Hall	£6 0s 0d
David Margot	£7 0s 0d
Trustees of Blacknall's charity for Abingdon St Nicolas	£10 10s 0d

It appears that the rights to other rectoral tithes had been acquired by the owners of the land in question and their value was collected as part of the rent.

In the latter half of the nineteenth century, Crockford's Clerical Directory gives the annual gross income of Radley's vicar as being £75 plus his house, very consistent with the 1849 tithe award of £70. To provide some comparison, the average agricultural labourer's wage at this time was around £30. Perhaps more revealing is a comparison with other incumbents in the area at that time (Table 6.1). It can be seen how little relationship there was between size of parish and pay, and how Radley vicars had by a clear margin the lowest income per church attender.

Table 6.1: Annual income of incumbents in the Radley area, 1872

Parish	Income (£)	Congregation (Sunday morning)	Income per head of congregation (£)
Marcham	455	109	4.2
Sunningwell	390	91	4.3
Cumnor	300	70	4.3
Drayton	130	60	2.2
Kennington	92	47	2.0
Radley	**75**	**100**	**0.7**

Source: Crockford's Clerical Directory 1872, congregation numbers from the 1851 religious census

We know that in neighbouring Oxfordshire only about 10% of incumbents at the same time had incomes of less than £100. Comparison with Trollope's fictional Barsetshire parishes is also revealing. When Josiah Crawley was incumbent at Hogglestock, his income was insufficient to feed and clothe his family adequately. His fortunes were transformed when he moved from there to the more agreeable parish of St Ewold, which had an annual income of

£350. But even the low paying Hogglestock had an annual income of £130, significantly more than that of Radley.

Radley was therefore a very poorly endowed parish by contemporary standards and its vicars would have needed other incomes, as indeed many had as is detailed in Chapter 5.

Today tithes and other historical endowments are irrelevant. Vicars in the Church of England all receive a stipend from their diocese, with very little variation in its level. In 2015-16 the national benchmark stipend was £24,690 plus housing costs. Although parishes do not set the level of remuneration, under the 'Parish Share' system they have to meet most if not all of the cost.

Bequests in wills

The large collection of will transcripts in Radley History Club's archives tell us much about how those facing their maker gave money both to the Church and to the poor, and how the pattern of giving changed over time.

Sixteenth century husbandmen and yeomen

The earliest wills in the archives are those of husbandmen and yeomen; people who might work 30 acres or so but who were not by any means rich. Bequests were frequently made to the diocese (at that time Sarum or Salisbury), to Radley Church itself, and to the poor of the village. The going rate to the diocese seems to have been 2d, and these payments have the look of an informal tax or even an insurance premium to safeguard the soul. The payments to Radley's church and poor were different in kind as they were within the community.

It is uncertain whether the bequests to the poor were distributed by the Church or through the poor law arrangements being put in place at this time. Examples of some of these bequests are given below.

> Thomas Porter of Thrupp: 1544
>
> I bequeath to the master church of Sarum 2d. I bequeath to the high altar within the chapel of Radley a bushel of barley.
>
> Harry White: 1557
>
> I give to the mother church of Sarum 2d. I give to the high altar in Radley church 4d. I give to the maintenance of the bells in Radley church one bushel of barley.
>
> Helen Porter, widow: 1557/8
>
> I give and bequeath to my mother church of Sarum two pence, to the high altar of my said parish church four pence, to the poor man's box four pence.

Richard Sheen of Thrupp: 1558

I bequeath to the mother church of Sarum 2d. I bequeath to the high altar of Radley church 2 bushels of wheat and to the church of Radley a quarter of barley. And to the bell of Radley 2 bushels of barley.

Thomas Porter of Thrupp: 1611/2

I give unto the poor people within Radley viz. 6d unto every married couple that have now no growing of their own and such as have been relieved by the parish heretofore.

Margery White: 1631

I do ordain that my executor hereafter named shall give and bestow at the time of my burial upon the poor people of the parish of Radley five shillings in bread.

Seventeenth and eighteenth century wills of people of means

As we move further into the seventeenth century we have examples of wills of people with greater means. The sums given are much larger and the payments are less formulaic, and in some cases suggest a desire to be remembered as well as to give.

First there is John Turvey, still calling himself a yeoman, but an educated man of some means who was possibly the bailiff to the Stonhouse family.

John Turvey, alias Buckingham: 1673

I do give and bequeath unto the church of Radley my little bible and Bishop Hall's paraphrase of the bible. I do give and bequeath forty shillings to buy a black cloth to cover myself and other dead corpses of servants and poor people in Radley aforesaid when they are carried to the church to be buried. I do give to the poor people of Radley aforesaid twenty shillings to be given and distributed amongst them by my executors.

Then we have the wills of the Stonhouses themselves. The will of Sir William Stonhouse shows among other things the local respect in which the vicar, John Herbert, was held. Although a learned man, Herbert was poor and he and his children married into yeomen rather than gentry families (see Chapter 5), but he was regarded by the lord of the Manor as a friend.

Sir William Stonhouse: 1631/2

I give and bequeath to the poor of the parish of Radley Five pounds to be distributed amongst them as my executors shall think AND WHEREAS I procured of the Executors of Henry Greene Ten pounds AND of the Executors of Richard Goad Ten pounds more, who were both my Servants, the said Twenty pounds intended to be employed to the use and benefit of the poor of Radley which accordingly hath been done NOW my Will is that my heirs & Executors take into their care that the said Twenty pounds be put into the hands of sufficient men with sureties that the yearly use and profit thereof according to the Statute be distributed to the poor according to the true meaning of the Donors.

I give twenty pounds more to the poor of the parish of Radley, praying that my Executors would put forth the same for their use after the rate beforesaid AND that they have care that the consideration money be paid yearly to the poor which amounteth to Three pounds and four shillings which four shillings being odd money were fit to be given to the Clerk for his pains in attendance at the Church.

I give to the poor of the parish of St. Helens in Abingdon Twenty pounds to be employed by the Mayor and Burgesses of the said Town towards a Stock to set poor people on work, that thereby they may be the better restrained from wandering abroad to steal wood or break hedges, and to commit such unlawful acts.

I give to my friend Mr. John Herbert the one moiety of the Tithe White[4] of Radley in as ample manner as is granted to me by the King's Letters Patent ALSO I give unto him Forty Shillings as a token of my love besides such duties belonging unto him by reason of his interest in the Tithes belonging to the Vicarage of Radley.

The will of his son Sir George Stonhouse seems concerned with reputation and includes explicit instructions to the vicar as to how this was to be secured, with payment to him conditional on compliance.

Sir George Stonhouse: 1674/5

I give unto six poor people and their families that are dwelling in the town of Radley one quarter of wheat to be delivered unto them at such times and in such manner as shall herein be directed First that six families be annually appointed by my executors and that they be such poor as pay not hearth money nor by the law ought to pay that duty And afterwards to be continued by my son John for ever Secondly that this gift be distributed according to the poor's necessities not all with a like proportion Thirdly that it be delivered at three several times in the year (viz.) at or against Christmas Easter and Whitsuntide notice being given to them to fetch it And for the more complete performance thereof I give to the Vicar of Radley forty shillings per annum conditionally that he do annually at the three abovesaid several times in his prayer in the pulpit before his service make commemoration and remembrance thereof by giving thanks for the gift after such manner and form as followeth (viz.) Given by Sir George Stonhouse Baronet Dame Margaret his wife daughter of Richard Lord Lovelace Baron of Hurley and John Stonhouse his son and heir And so to be continued by him and remain for ever Upon the vicars omission thereof this gift of forty shillings to cease.

As we move into the eighteenth century, reputation seems to reckon even larger in the will of Martha Stonhouse.

---

[4] This is an oddity as it implies that Stonhouse received the little tithes himself. His letters patent of 1560 gave him no rights to tithes previously held by Abingdon Abbey, which the Crown appears to have sold separately. The Stonhouses might have purchased them, but little tithes were anyway held by the vicar of St Helen's rather than the Abbey.

Dame Martha Stonhouse: 1703/4

… expending thereout the sum of two hundred pounds in erecting a monument in memory of my late husband and myself in Radley Church And also being at the sole charges of my funeral and burial in Radley Church aforesaid which I compute at one hundred pounds but leave the expense thereof to his discretion.

To the poor of Radley ten pounds to be disposed amongst them at my funeral in such proportions as my said son Sir John shall direct.

Nineteenth century wills establishing charitable trusts

Of particular interest in the nineteenth century are the wills of John Davis, a landowner and farmer (1820),[5] and Martha Bristow née Langford of Pumney Farm (1876).[6] Extracts from both wills are recorded in memorial plaques in the south aisle of Radley Church (Figures 6.1 and 6.2).

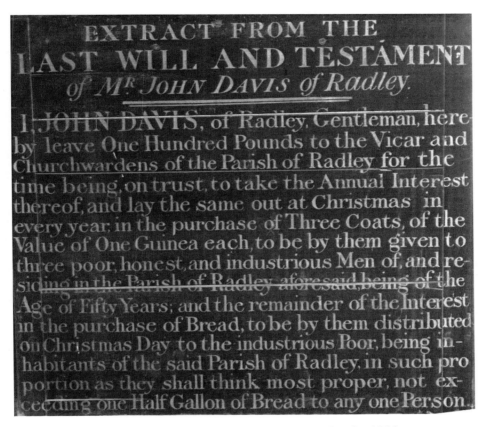

Figure 6.1: Extract from will of John Davis, 1820

---

[5] John Davis, son of Gabriel and Elizabeth Davis, farmed at Church Farm directly opposite the Church.

[6] Martha was the daughter of John and Anne Langford of Pumney Farm. She was born in 1804 and married Joseph Bristow in 1826.

Figure 6.2: Extract from the will of Martha Bristow, 1876

Unlike the other wills we have seen, these created ongoing charities to be administered by the Church. Bequests of this kind were not unusual at this time and numerous examples can be found in the Victoria County History.[7] We look at the administration of these two charities later in this chapter.

Churchwardens' accounts

We are fortunate that detailed churchwardens' accounts exist for each year from 1739 to 1904-05. These show routine expenditure, larger one-off items and sources of income, all of which provide insights into Church and village life at the time. There were some significant changes over the period covered, both as to items of expenditure and to sources of income.

In the eighteenth century, expenditure in a normal year was typically about £5. Regular items covered various aspects of the routine running of the Church such as the purchase of communion bread and wine, the washing of vestments, cleaning equipment and the clerk's fees. They also covered the cost of the visitation dinner, which was typically about 15s. This dinner was given as part of the annual inspection by the archdeacon and was clearly a significant event in the calendar. An annual payment of 5s was also made to the vicar of St Helen's Abingdon. This sum was described in 1783 by the vicar of St Helen's as a 'trifling acknowledgement' of his responsibility for Radley, which existed by then in form only, but not in practice. These payments continued until 1864-65.

A more curious recurring item first made its appearance in 1779. This was the killing of sparrows, for which payment was made by the dozen. In that year 4s 0d was paid for 24½

---

[7] The Victoria History of the Counties of England, a local history publishing project begun in 1899 and dedicated to Queen Victoria.

dozen. The peak year was 1826 when a remarkable 325 dozen were killed at a cost of £4 1s 3d. It appears from one year's entry that the payments were made to the boys of the village. For such sums to have been spent the sparrows must have been a serious nuisance. They may well have roosted in the ivy, with which the Church was largely covered at this time (Figure 6.3). However, evidence from other parishes suggests that the payments were more to do with the wider parish than the Church itself and there was a particular concern about sparrows scavenging grain.

Figure 6.3: Radley Church *c*.1890
The ivy may have been home to sparrows, which were regarded as a major nuisance. The churchwardens paid a bounty for each dozen sparrows killed.

By the mid nineteenth century, expenditure in a normal year had risen to about £15-20. The nature of the expenditure also begins to change around this time, less on the church itself and more on the wider welfare of the village. In 1835-36 payments began to the village school: initially five guineas, rising to 10 guineas from 1855-56. In 1870-71 payments began to the 'sick and poor' of the village. Initially we are only given totals (£9 5s 6d in that first year) but by the 1890s individual payments are itemised. By the turn of the century, payments were also beginning to appear for wider charitable causes beyond the village. This increasing engagement with charitable giving is considered later in this chapter.

In some years the accounts show that more substantial one-off expenditure was incurred – invariably on the physical fabric of the Church. Some of these items are described in more detail in Chapters 2 and 3.

- In 1754, expenditure was £62 3s 7d, of which £51 4s 0½d was on five new bells for the Church commissioned from Abel Rudhall of Gloucester.

- In 1775, expenditure was £89 16s 7d, the largest items being replacement of church seats and repair of the church roof.

- In 1801, £8 9s 3d was spent erecting and furnishing a new gallery for the Church. This was almost certainly associated with music and the accounts show that shortly afterwards a 'singing master' was engaged. In 1808 the singing master was Mr West, who was paid £8 15s 0d.

- In 1812-13, Mr Goodluck was paid £44 0s 4d, mainly it seems for painting, varnishing and re-leading of windows, and more general sprucing up rather than new items.

- In 1852-53, Mr Roberts was paid £48 10s 6d for erecting a new churchyard fence.

- In 1855-56, £22 was spent on a refurbishment and rehanging of the church bells.

- In 1891-92, David Stroud was paid £11 for repairing the chancel window.

How was all this expenditure financed? Up until the 1860s it almost all came from the church rate. This was an annual levy on all ratepayers in the parish, alongside the rate which they paid separately to the overseers of the poor. The church rate was controversial in some parishes, and also at national level, because it was levied on all ratepayers regardless of whether they were adherents of the Church of England. This was particularly resented where there were large numbers of non-conformists. We know that Albon Bradshaw, a Roman Catholic, was reported by the churchwardens in 1695 for not paying the church rate on Wick Farm. However, refusal to pay does not appear to have been a significant issue in Radley.

In 1868 the Compulsory Church Rate Abolition Act was passed. It appears from Radley's accounts that no attempt was made to levy an equivalent voluntary rate and there was therefore a significant change in the financing of church spending. In 1870-71, the accounts show that income was just over £25. Of this £2 5s 8d was a grant from St Peter's [Radley] College, which henceforth became a regular item. The remainder was from 'offertories' or church collections.

This change was not just a matter of accounting, but effectively a separation at local level of church and state. Radley Church was now reliant for finance on its congregation, and also on its patron, rather than on the village at large. As the village grew and congregations as a percentage of the village fell, this became increasingly significant.

Gifts and fundraising

Not all major spending on the Church has passed through the churchwardens' accounts. There have been significant gifts, especially from the Church's patron, and increasingly there have been major fundraising exercises.

The patron of a church is the holder of the advowson, or the right to appoint the vicar (see Chapter 5). For most of the nineteenth century, the patronage was held by the Bowyer family, who were also lords of the manor, and they made significant gifts. In the 1840s, George Bowyer (1810-1883)[8] donated the fine carved choir stalls which came from Cologne and date to about 1600, and also the heraldic stained glass which was made or restored by Thomas Willement (see Chapter 3). In 1897, Miss Mary Bowyer gave to the vicar and churchwardens a plot of land to the east of the Church; the existing school house was already on this plot and it was additionally used for the extension of the churchyard and, in the early 1980s, the building of the Church Room (see Chapter 2).

In 1902, Mrs Josephine Dockar-Drysdale, who had purchased most of the Bowyer's estate (see Chapter 1), paid for the large timber arches placed across the nave roof as part of the restoration of that year.

Radley College, which purchased the advowson from the Bowyers in 1867, has also been very active in its patronage. It was, for example, the College which built the Victorian extension to the Vicarage in 1869 at a cost of £500. It might be assumed that the Bowyers and Radley College were wealthy and easily able to make these gifts, but that is not the case. The Bowyer family lost most of its money from a failed project to mine coal in Bayworth in 1812 to 1813, and the College was deeply in debt at the time it extended the Vicarage.

From the end of the nineteenth century to the present day, all major enhancements and restorations have been paid for primarily by fundraising appeals. The first, and probably the largest of these appeals, was for the major restoration of 1902, which was launched in 1899 and ran through to 1904. It raised £1,532 7s 10½d. In parallel, a separate appeal raised £183 3s 6d for the restoration in 1903 of the organ in memory of Dr Edwin Monk (see Chapter 3). In 1952 an appeal raised £400 to finance a rehanging of the bells. In 2008-09, £180,000 was raised to deal with the devastation caused by death watch beetle. Most recently an appeal in 2015 raised a remarkable £33,500 in a single June weekend towards the £37,000 cost of the repair of the Church bells.

Promoting these appeals became a major pre-occupation of the incumbents at the time and they were most successful when they fully engaged the wider village community. Some flavour of what is involved is found in Chapter 2, where there is a full description of the appeals for the 1902 restoration and the 2008 to 2009 beetle restoration.

Helping the poor of the village

We have seen from wills that Radley Church has helped the poor of the village for as long as records survive. This role seems, however, to have developed in particular in the nineteenth century. It is possible that this reflects changes in poor law legislation. Under the 'old' Poor Law of 1601, a poor rate was levied and Radley had its own overseer of the poor, who in practice had some discretion as to how the poor were helped. Under the 'new' Poor Law of 1834 the poor rate continued but local discretion was reduced; parishes were also brigaded into larger 'unions', each with its own workhouse. In 1835 Radley became part of the

---

[8] He inherited the title in 1860 on the death of his father, Sir George Bowyer, who was the patron but was living abroad at the time of these gifts to the Church.

Abingdon Poor Law Union and a new workhouse was built there. It is possible that the Church became more active partly to re-introduce a more local connection between the village's poor and their assistance.

Initially the Church's role in helping the poor seems primarily to have been in the distribution of funds provided by local benefactors. The Davis and Bristow charities (financed by the bequests mentioned earlier in this chapter) were both administered by the vicar and churchwardens (after 1894 by the vicar and members of the Parochial Church Council). It is likely that the Church also had a role in distributing the Christmas gifts to the poor provided by the Bowyer family. The parish registers contain very detailed information on all these distributions and they provide considerable insight into the village at the time.

Davis charity (from 1821)

The Davis charity provided for the distribution of three coats each year to 'poor, honest and industrious men' aged 50 and above. In 1849 it was decided to lower the age limit to 40 because:

> experience has proved that candidates for the coats above 50 years of age, and if the proper qualifications [are met] in other respects, are not as found.

In 1854, the limit was restored to 50 years because of fears about departing from the terms of the will but the vicar, Robert Gibbings (see Chapter 5), personally funded a coat for Henry Weston whom he regarded as particularly deserving although aged under 50.

Throughout the nineteenth century, the interest from the initial £100 was enough to purchase three coats each year and sometimes four, but from 1913 only two coats could be afforded and from 1917 only one. The last recorded donation, to a Mr King of Sugworth, was in 1935.

Bristow charity (from 1879)

The Bristow charity was in many ways similar, but the will left much more discretion to the Church as to who should receive donations and in what form. It was decided to make the annual distribution in the form of blankets, although on one occasion (1901) shawls and a rug were given instead. There was no limitation by age or gender. In some years the ages of recipients are given and these suggest a bias towards the elderly. There is an interesting note in 1901 that the award to H. Badnell was:

> given by some mistake to G. Badnell, who keeps it, knowing it was meant for his father.

The interest from the £150 bequest was initially enough to purchase 15 blankets each winter at a cost of £4 5s 6d. In 1914, this fell to 12 'owing to war prices' and there were further falls to five by 1917. With some small variation this number was maintained until 1935 when the last entry appears in the parish registers (as with the Davis charity). It is possible that some donations were made after 1935, but no record of this survives.

Bowyer gifts (1840 to 1850)

The Bowyer donations differ in that they were lifetime gifts, not an ongoing charity. The parish registers contain entries only between 1840 and 1850, and it is not known whether any were made outside this period. Other than the 1848 donations of coal, all were at Christmas and all by Sir George Bowyer (1783-1860). He owned most of the village but lived on the continent. The 1848 coal donation was by his brother, the Revd Henry Bowyer of Sunningwell.

In 1840 the Bowyers donated three scarlet cloaks and six brown cloaks, all to women. There were similar donations of cloaks to women in each of the next three years. The limitation to women might have been deliberate to offset the limitation of the Davis charity to men. There was also a donation of 24 blankets in 1842 and 12 blankets in 1843, mainly to men.

In 1848, and the next three years, there were donations of 'beef for Christmas'. The number of recipients varied between 59 and 64, and this must have accounted for all or nearly all of the labouring households in the village. The amounts per household varied from 2 to 12 lb, presumably reflecting the number of mouths to be fed.

In 1848, there was a donation of coal to 56 villagers, essentially the same people as received the beef. The quantities varied from 2 to 5 cwt (approximately 100 to 250 kg).

Recipients

The same family names appear repeatedly among the recipients of these charitable schemes. The Davis charity made 13 gifts of cloaks to members of the Gibbins, Minns and Woodley families, 10 to the Bennetts and Comleys, and nine to the Hooks and Villebois's. James Woodley received a cloak in four separate years. The Bristow charity made 41 gifts of blankets to the Villebois's, 37 to the Gibbins, 32 to the Woodleys and 29 to the Comleys. The tradition appears to have been that the recipients were announced during the service on Christmas Day and they then collected the gifts on Boxing Day.

Viewed from the twenty-first century, it is difficult to assess how charitable gifts in kind of this type were regarded at the time. There can be little doubt that there was much hardship in Radley. The censuses show that a significant number were in receipt of poor relief and unemployment rose during the agricultural depression towards the end of the century. Homes would be cold and anything to keep people warm must have been welcome. The gifts were probably deliberately made in kind to avoid cash being frittered away. No one could have objected to getting free coal as this was a necessity needing otherwise to be bought – but coats and blankets? So many were given that one wonders whether some might have been sold on in some kind of secondary market. Might there also have been some stigma about wearing a charity coat?

Radley Church's changing role

In the last 30 years of the nineteenth century, the churchwardens' accounts show that the Church became directly involved in poor relief, distributing money it had itself collected rather than just acting as the agent of charitable funds established by other benefactors. The Church's annual expenditure on the poor, about £8 to £10, was significant and about the same as the combined annual distributions from the Davis and Bristow charities. The nature and pattern of the expenditure was different. Payments were made in cash not in kind, and they were more sustained – not just one-off Christmas gifts. The accounts give details of individual recipients and some villagers (for example Widows Badnall, Bennett, Woodley, Dawson and Silvester) were receiving regular subventions from the Church of 6d or 1s a week. We have no record of the policy behind these distributions, but it may have been a deliberate departure from what might have seemed an increasingly outmoded form of poor assistance.

The Davis and Bristow charities still formally exist, but are in effect dormant with the funds available greatly diminished by inflation. It is currently envisaged that they will be wound up and the residual funds distributed in a form, such as food bank donations, which is in keeping with the original charitable purposes but with modern needs and circumstances in mind.

Wider charitable causes

The picture we have from the records is that the Church was at first primarily concerned with spending on its own essential maintenance and then later, from the mid nineteenth century, with the wider village and then, as we shall see, with wider causes beyond. There is however an interesting set of accounts, detailed below, which suggest that this is not the full story.

Donations to other churches in the eighteenth century

The parish registers give an interesting list of donations made to other churches across the country between 1722 and 1749. We do not know whether this is the only period for which there are records or whether donations were limited to this period. It is possible that this was a particular initiative of Nathaniel Thompson, who was vicar between 1716 and 1745 (see Chapter 5). The spending is not contained in the churchwardens' accounts and seems to have been a parallel account, funded by ad hoc donations and not by the church rate. Whatever the position, it is striking that Radley, arguably an insular farming community, extended its giving so broadly.

Some flavour is given by the entries for 1744 when 14 donations were made, ranging from 1s 6d to 4s 4d, and totalling £2 2s 3d in all. The recipient churches were as far afield as Devon, Montgomeryshire, Yorkshire and Kent. Six were stated to be for loss by fire, one by storm and one by floods. In the other cases it seems likely that there was a need for major repair from the ravages of time, a requirement that Radley itself had at the end of the nineteenth century.

In other years there tended to be fewer donations but some were larger. The largest was for £10 2s 10d in 1722, but the name of the church is illegible. The largest legible donation was to Cranbrook, Hertfordshire, for £1 2s 2d in 1727.

There is an interesting entry for 1726 as follows:

> Memo, The brief for loss by fire in Buckingham in ye Com' [County] of Buckingham was read July 10th. On ye 14th there was collected £0 2s 9d from howse to howse but it was lost afterwards by the churchwarden.

It seems that the Revd Nathaniel Thompson made up the loss himself. What happened to the original 2s 9d we do not know! The wording 'from howse to howse' is also interesting, providing confirmation that this expenditure was funded by voluntary donations and not by the church rate.

Hospitals, missions and Empire

In the last decade of the nineteenth century and the first of the twentieth, it is striking that giving by the Church begins to broaden in its horizons.

Locally money is now given not just to those within the village, but also to the hospitals in Abingdon and Oxford. Charities in London's East End also begin to feature. For example, the collection of £4 1s 10¼d from the harvest thanksgiving service in September 1895 was sent to the Radcliffe Infirmary in Oxford and Abingdon Cottage Hospital, as were the saleable offerings. The flowers were sent to east London. Missions in the wider Empire also begin to receive donations, including the Oxford Mission to Calcutta and the Zululand Mission. The latter received donations totalling over £6 in 1896-97.

It is likely that this wider approach to giving reflected the influence of Charles Gore and James Nash, who were vicars between 1893 and 1898 (see Chapter 5). The Community of the Resurrection to which they belonged was active in charitable work among the urban poor and also in missionary work in southern Africa.

In 1900, at the time of the Boer War, £2 12 0d was given to the Lord Mayor of London's War Fund.

Charitable giving today

Today's charitable giving by Radley Church is based on the principle of tithing. We have seen that in medieval times the vicar's income came largely from tithes, in cash and kind, whereby he received one tenth of the value of produce in the parish. That concept has now been turned right round by Radley Church so that each year it gives away one tenth of the income it receives.

The current income of Radley Church (from regular contributions, collections during services and miscellaneous sources such as hire of the Church Room) is sufficient to allow a tithe of some £4,500 to be distributed to charities. The policy is to support each year three main charities, typically international and Christian in their mission, with donations of about £1,200 each. These charities are also supported by prayer. Each receives support for three consecutive years, with one charity being rotated each year. In 2015-16 the recipients were:

- Christian Solidarity Worldwide;
- Church Mission Society;

- Jeel al Amal, a school in Palestine.

In addition, smaller donations of about £200 are given each year to about five charities with a more local base or connection, and which are not necessarily connected with the Church. In 2015-16 these were:

- Abingdon Food Bank;
- CLIC Sargent;
- Oxfordshire South and Vale Citizens Advice Bureau;
- Sobell House Hospice;
- St Luke's Healthcare for the Clergy.

Collections of non-perishable foods are also made for the Abingdon Food Bank once a month and parishioners have been involved with their distribution.

Lastly it is worth mentioning the Prayer Shawl, a joint initiative with Sunningwell and Kennington. Parishioners knit, and pray over, a beautiful shawl which is given to a local person in need. There are echoes here of the Bristow and Davis charities, but on a much more personalised and sensitive basis.

Sources

Tithes and the remuneration of incumbents

The information about Radley tithes is from:

> For 1272: *The Two Cartularies of Abingdon*, G. Lambrick and C.F. Slade, Volume 2, Oxford History Society New Series XXXIII, 1990
>
> For 1678: Radley Glebe Terrier, Wiltshire Record Office WRO D1/24/237/3
>
> For 1849: Tithe Award and Map, 1849, The National Archives, Award IR 29/2/101, Map 30/2/101

Vicars' salaries are from:

> Crockford's Clerical Directory 1872
>
> *Oxfordshire Clergy 1777-1869*, D. McClatchey, 1960
>
> *The Last Chronicle of Barset*, A. Trollope, 1867

Bequests in wills and other gifts

Radley History Club archives contain transcripts of the wills quoted from in this chapter.

Churchwardens' accounts

The accounts are held by the Berkshire Record Office (BRO) at BRO D/P95/5/1.

Gifts and fundraising

The same sources were consulted as those for the relevant building projects listed at the end of Chapter 2, plus *The History of Radley College 1847-1947*, A.K. Boyd, 1948.

Helping the poor of the village

All the information about the Davis and Bristow charities and the gifts from the Bowyers is taken from: 'Radley, St. James, Berkshire, Parish Registers' [Baptisms 1599-1950 – Marriages 1599-1961 – Banns 1761-1830, 1881-1895 – Burials 1599-1950 – Appendices], transcribed by Fiona Hedges and Irene Littleby, Oxfordshire Family History Society, 1996

Direct assistance by the Church is taken from the churchwardens' accounts.

Wider charitable causes

All the information about donations to other churches in the eighteenth century is taken from: 'Radley, St. James, Berkshire, Parish Registers' [Baptisms 1599-1950 – Marriages 1599-1961 – Banns 1761-1830, 1881-1895 – Burials 1599-1950 – Appendices], transcribed by Fiona Hedges and Irene Littleby, Oxfordshire Family History Society, 1996

Donations to wider causes between 1890 and 1910 are taken from the churchwardens' accounts.

Policy on giving today is based on information from members of Radley Parochial Church Council.

Photographs courtesy of Les Hemsworth (the charity monuments) and Radley History Club archives (Radley Church, *c.*1890)

Chapter 7: The Church Today and the Role of the Laity

by Pam McKellen and Tony Rogerson

A perusal of the guidebooks in many churches would lead one to conclude that the church is all about the building and the clergy. Most people tend to think of Radley Church as the 'building on the corner'. But the word church (ecclesia) means 'an assembly' or 'called-out ones'. The church then is the body of believers. The universal church refers to all believers who have ever lived. The local church is those believers living in a particular place today.

Clergy make up only a small fragment of the local church. The vast majority who worship Sunday by Sunday are the laity – laity from the Greek word 'laos' or 'people' – and denotes all who are not ordained as clergy. Their role in the local church is not only as the body of worshippers, but also in the running and maintenance of the church in numerous different capacities. These range from officiating in non-sacramental services (licensed lay ministers), reading lessons, leading prayers, singing in the choir and bell-ringing, to looking after the church finances, making sure building repairs are carried out, cleaning the church, tending the graveyards, making coffee after services, and a hundred and one other routine but essential tasks.

The role of the laity has become increasingly important over the last century or so. Currently at St James the Great in Radley, about 90 lay people contribute to looking after the Church, its grounds and its services.

Within the scope of this book, it would be impossible to do justice to the numerous lay people who have served 'St James' down the ages. So this chapter focuses only on the laity of today. It begins by setting the scene with an outline of the regular programme of activities at the Church. It then describes some of the roles carried out by laity. Several of the current lay office holders describe what they do from their own perspective. This is supplemented by additional information where appropriate.

Church services and activities for members

St James currently has three services on Sundays. At 8 am we hold a Book of Common Prayer communion service. The 11 am main service is a Common Worship communion service, except on the first Sunday of the month. On that day we hold an informal 'Messy Church' service. For this all the pews are pushed back and we have many activities for the children and a café area for adults to have coffee, with a short service at the end.

The evening service at 6 pm varies on a monthly cycle. The first Sunday is a Communion, the second, Reflect@6, the third a sung Book of Common Prayer (BCP) evensong and the fourth a reflective Iona service. This way people can choose their own Sunday evening programme! On the occasional fifth Sunday, there is a Songs of Praise for all the churches in the benefice. 'Reflect@6' is not a service but a talk by a Christian about what they do – such as an MP, surgeon or aid worker – or about an interesting topic such as Street Pastors, cosmology or the Citizens Advice Bureau.

Messy Church

There are many mid-week activities, including four Home Groups where the Bible is studied and issues of faith discussed. On Monday and Thursday, Morning Prayer is said and on Saturday morning there is a prayer meeting. Many Church members are also involved with the Prayer Triplets: meeting with two others to pray. Every Friday morning a café, known as Café Radley, is held in the Church Room. There is a monthly Women's Fellowship meeting and a Prayer Shawl Group meets regularly. A men's group loosely connected with the Church is involved in a number of activities including a monthly meeting in the Bowyer Arms and a quarterly Saturday morning breakfast with a talk and discussion.

Total attendances at the three services on normal Sundays, excluding major festivals, range between 60 and 110.

Licensed lay ministers

Licensed lay ministers (LLMs) (previously known as 'lay readers' or just 'readers') are lay people who are licensed to preach, teach and lead worship. There are currently more than 10,000 active LLMs in the Church of England. Most are licensed to a parish but some are chaplains in prisons, hospitals, hospices or schools. They give their services to the church so do not receive payment. The office of lay reader as it was then called came into being in 1866. Women were first licensed to the role during the First World War due to the shortage of men.

Sue Sowden started training as a reader in 1991, inspired initially by a woman lay reader in her church. Following two years of training she was licensed in 1993 to her parish church in Horspath. In 1994 she became head of St Mary's School, Wantage. In this role she fulfilled her reader duties within the school and in its chapel. Her ministry involved helping with the school services and also a wide-ranging pastoral role with the girls.

'Following my retirement as a reader in Wantage in 2006 I became a reader, renamed more recently LLM, in the benefice of Radley and Sunningwell. Until recently I have been in paid employment and my ministry has been primarily exercised on Sundays. I have been taking Morning Prayer and Evensong, have led in the first part of Communion service, preached and led intercessions in all three churches in the benefice. I have also been a regular server, assisting the clergy at communions. I am hoping perhaps now to make a wider contribution.

I very much value my work as an LLM. Practically it enables me to help the clergy team with the quite heavy load of services in the now united benefice of Radley, Sunningwell and Kennington. I feel I am able to make a contribution to the spiritual life of the benefice and as a lay person can bring a different perspective to this. I feel I am in the place which God has called me to. I enjoy exercising my ministry and I relish preparing sermons and preaching them.'

The other LLM, Martha Young, has served in the Church since 2003, where her smile and wide-ranging interests have endeared her to many.

'When I worshipped in my church in Coventry, I explored ways in which I could best serve God. My vicar helped me decide to seek to become a reader and I began two years' training in 1995 and was licensed as a lay minister in 1997. I moved back to Oxfordshire in 2003 and settled in Radley. I began to attend St James and had my LLM licence transferred to the Oxford Diocese. At first I was very nervous as Radley was very different to my previous parish. However, people were very welcoming and I soon settled in. I have enjoyed preaching and taking services here, including the monthly Songs of Praise, for the past 13 years.

My father, who died when I was 10, taught me to question everything. When I preach I hope to encourage people to think and question. I don't mind if they disagree with me. I am very happy to discuss any subject because we all learn from each other's experiences.'

Tower captain

One of the joys of a village church like St James the Great is the peal of bells which calls worshippers to the main Sunday morning service and greets the newly married couple as they come out from the church. Information on the bells and their history is given in Chapter 3.

Bell-ringing is a skill for which careful training is needed and it is pre-eminently a team effort. The trainer and leader of the team of bell-ringers is called the tower captain. Daphne Pollard has been the tower captain since 1995, but her association with the bells in St James goes back to 1953. As a school girl at Radley Primary School she was introduced to bell-ringing by the head, Miss Cross, who was also the then tower captain. Many girls had a go at bell-ringing but did not continue. Daphne took to it like a duck to water and has been ringing in the Church now for 62 years, taking over as tower captain when the redoubtable Miss Cross retired.

'My responsibilities involve organising the weekly ringing at the 11 am Sunday services and the Thursday evening practices. I train the new bell-ringers and am the point of contact for ringing on other occasions such as weddings and funerals. I also organise the ringing, usually of a quarter peal, on special occasions such as Remembrance Sunday or events like the Queen's Jubilee.

We are fortunate in Radley to have a good number of ringers. Some other churches are finding it hard to get enough. Our current age range of ringers goes from 12 to 82. Mid-teens is a good age to learn to ring and at that time it probably takes a few months to get a person to the point of being able to ring on a Sunday. Older folk may take a year to do so but it is great that people of all ages can ring together. Of course there is always more to learn as I still find after all these years as a ringer. It is one of the joys of bell-ringing.

The bells need annual maintenance by outside bell-hangers and occasionally need more serious attention. In the autumn of 2015, the bells were taken away for major repair and were back by Christmas. It is a tribute to how meaningful the bells are that the £35,000 needed for these repairs was raised in a single weekend by the generous gifts of very many people in Radley.

From time to time outsiders come to ring the bells at St James. Some of our bell-ringers also go to other churches to ring there. No two peals of bells are ever the same. I count myself privileged to be tower captain and love what I do.'

Churchwardens

Wardens are unpaid lay officials who play a key role in the running of a church. Many current lay duties are comparatively recent, but the office of churchwarden dates from the thirteenth century and is thus one of the earliest forms of recognised lay ministry. The primary function of the office at that time seems to have been that of taking care of the church building and its contents. Over the years since then other duties have been added.

As will be evident in other chapters of this book, churchwardens' records are a vital way of tracing the history of the church. Historically there were two types of wardens: the 'people's warden' chosen by the parishioners and the 'rector's warden' chosen by the incumbent. The distinction no longer exists but there are always two wardens, elected by the parishioners at the Annual Parochial Church Meeting.

Wardens have what is called a wand or stave. These were originally sharp-pointed sticks to prod people or dogs and were known as 'prodders' in the 1600s. The purpose of the prodding, at least as far as people are concerned, is not quite clear. The thought that they were used to keep people awake during sermons is apocryphal. Later they were used in processions as symbols of the wardens' authority. Some churches still use them in this way. Others like Radley Church no longer do so.

Below, one of today's churchwardens, Iain Winton (previously an IT consultant with Esso but now retired), describes the various elements of the role.

'I was really a non-believer for many years, but after my wife's death five years ago, I began my journey of faith which led to my attending St James. I have never been one for passive involvement and am a very practical person and like to use my hands. There was a vacancy as a warden and I allowed my name to go forward and was elected at the Annual Parochial Church Meeting and took up my duties in May 2013.

As a warden I have a legal responsibility to represent the parishioners' interests to the vicar. I have the right, fortunately not so far used, to eject unruly people from the Church and to arrest anyone abusing the Church or church land. On weekdays my responsibilities centre round helping to make sure the Church and Church Room are properly maintained. On Sundays in conjunction with my fellow warden I check that all is ready for the running of the services and for welcoming people. A warden is present at every service. If there is an interregnum, wardens play a large part in helping to draw up the parish profile and in choosing a new vicar.

My duties take up about a day and a half each week, plus three hours or more on Sundays. It is therefore quite time-consuming, but I feel I can help lift loads of practical work from the shoulders of the clergy.

There have been some unusual things which I have been called upon to do. I have had the perilous job of clearing the Church roof gutters with my fellow warden. I have had to unblock the toilets in the Church Room and to seek to locate a leak of water in the tower vestry. However, I find it a worthwhile role and particularly fulfilling when the Church is full to overflowing at a major festival and all goes smoothly.'

Treasurer

This is one of the key roles and involves the handling of the Church's finances. The present treasurer is David Handscomb, who was a lecturer in mathematics at Oxford University before retiring.

'I was elected as treasurer in April 2006. It is a varied job. I handle and keep records of the income and expenditure of the Church, including the expenses of the vicar. I deal with donations made with Gift Aid and reclaim the tax from HM Revenue & Customs – all done online now. I also ensure the money is banked week by week.

I provide the annual budget and I am responsible to the Parochial Church Council for giving the financial information that is needed for appropriate decisions to be made, including for unusual expenditure. I present the annual statement of accounts to the Parochial Church Council and the Annual Parochial Church Meeting. I receive the fees paid for weddings and funerals. No charge is made for baptisms. I handle all insurance matters regarding the Church and the Church Room.

There are times when my job is a busy one, not least at the end of each month with the reconciling of the bank statement and also at end of each financial year. However, I feel it is a privilege to do this job with its significant responsibilities. I feel I am able to use some of the gifts God has given me to serve the church.'

Parochial Church Council

The Parochial Church Council (PCC) is the executive committee of a Church of England parish and consists of the clergy and churchwardens together with representatives of the laity. Its principal mission, as defined in the PCC (Powers) Measure 1956, is to 'promote in the parish the whole mission of the church'.

Legally, the PCC is responsible for the financial affairs of the church and the maintenance of its assets such as the church and church hall. The PCC replaced the old vestry committee in 1921. The PCC is a charity and its members are all trustees.

PCC secretary

The current PCC secretary is Yvonne Milward, who before retiring was a practice manager in a nearby GP practice.

'I became PCC secretary in 2011 when I was appointed by the PCC. I have to be reappointed each year. The PCC deals with a variety of matters including: building maintenance and repairs; church services and activities; approval of budgets and other financial decisions; and making sure the graveyards are kept in good order.

The PCC meets every eight weeks or so. My role is first to make sure that the Standing Committee (vicar, wardens, treasurer and myself) meets about a week before each PCC meeting. For the PCC meeting itself I send out the agenda, book the Church Room, and take and then distribute the minutes.

The Annual Parochial Church Meeting takes place in March or April. Everyone on the electoral register of Radley Church is allowed to attend and vote on the appointment of PCC members and to receive reports on all the Church activities and Church finances. It is a time when the Church officers and PCC members are accountable to the Church members. The Annual Church Parochial Meeting is a busy time for me in getting reports from all the Church organisations and making arrangements for the electing of PCC members, as well as the sending out of the agenda and taking the minutes.

The job of PCC secretary is the kind of role which was part of my work as a practice manager, but I find it a challenge to make sure that everything is done accurately. I get a great feeling of satisfaction when I can look back after a PCC meeting or the Annual Church Parochial Meeting and find that things have gone smoothly and been done well.'

PCC members

One of the current PCC members is Emma Moore, who works in a GP practice as a clinical auditor.

'I was asked by the vicar to let my name go forward and was voted on to the PCC at the Annual Church Parochial Meeting in 2010. As a member of the PCC, I attend the bimonthly meetings and join in the discussions and decisions on the wide variety of matters brought before us. I am also currently the vice-chair and carry out that duty if the vicar is not available.

The PCC plays an important part in running the Church and in representing the parishioners in decision-making. We have a responsibility to make sure that the income and expenditure of the Church is handled well. I find it is not a particularly time-consuming role but one which needs good preparation before each meeting. I enjoy making a contribution to the Church in this way and appreciate the camaraderie experienced in our midst.'

Vicar's secretary

To help her with some of her many administrative responsibilities, the vicar has a part-time secretary. Katie North, previously a bank cashier, took on this role in 2005 shortly after Pam McKellen arrived.

'I work three mornings a week in the office in the Vicarage. I see my job as supporting the vicar with the paperwork and much of the day-to-day 'nitty-gritty' matters which need dealing with. I help prepare the service sheet with the hymns on it for the main Sunday service. I am the first point of contact for wedding requests and deal with the initial paperwork. I arrange the dates on which the banns of marriage will be read. I organise the venue and invitations for the annual Wedding Preparation Day, when couples are helped to prepare for their marriage. I also get the written material together for that day.

I am also the first point of contact for baptisms and deal with the paperwork involved. We have several Baptism Preparation evenings a year and I help to organise these. It is not part of my role as vicar's secretary but I am also one of the Baptism Link Team. This means that I am present at some of the baptisms and participate in them. Thereafter I keep in touch with the parents.

I am not too much involved with funerals, though I am the point of contact when the vicar is away. I have plans of the three Church graveyards on my computer with the details of who is buried where, which I update following an interment. When the vicar is away I handle all phone calls and correspondence coming into the Vicarage, and pass matters onto the appropriate people when necessary.

Generally I enjoy my job, working as I do for a good and understanding boss, particularly my involvement with people. However, I always find it hard when people ring about a bereavement. On the other hand, weddings and baptisms are happy events and it is a privilege to be involved with these.'

Music at Radley Church

For hundreds of years music in churches has been provided by musicians, especially organists and choristers, often accompanied by instruments ranging from shawms[1] and recorders to the wide variety of other things in recent years.

The organ (described in Chapter 3) has been the mainstay of music in the Church and the coming of David Beckett as organist in 1972 changed the face of worship. Helen Beckett commented: 'When he arrived, there was a small choir consisting of four or five singers. By recruiting children from the village, the primary school and Radley College, the choir grew to a good size'. The choir would meet on Friday evenings for choir practice and bit by bit adults

---

[1] A double-reed woodwind instrument, popular during the Middle Ages and the Renaissance.

joined – often the parents of the children – and the lively, enthusiastic choir grew. The choristers enjoyed an eclectic range of music from psalms, chants and responses to music for special concerts. One chorister commented: 'I started coming to church because of the choir and became a Christian. I learnt to appreciate choral music in a way that has only continued to enrich my life'.

David affiliated the Church to the Royal School of Church Music (RSCM) and many of the choir would join in its choir festivals, with some of the younger ones also going to the annual RSCM three-day course in the Easter holidays in Oxford. These ended with a special evensong in Christ Church Cathedral sung by choristers selected from the attendees. David encouraged particularly talented choristers to study for the RSCM Bishop's Awards (successful candidates wear their medal on a distinctive purple ribbon) and he spent many hours rehearsing and encouraging them. Choir members enjoyed outings to the seaside and the pantomime in Oxford, and at Christmas sang carols round the village. These things continued for many years. The 'yellow' hymn book – both loved and hated (!) – was produced in 2003 and introduced newer hymns that had not previously been included in the Church's repertoire.

The heyday of the choir was probably in the 1990s. After that, recruitment became more difficult. Today, we have a smaller choir but one that is still competent and loyal, and very committed to leading worship each Sunday and singing a set evensong each month. On special occasions like Christmas, others who love singing but are not able to join a regular choir have been part of an augmented choir and have enjoyed contributing to the worship.

Over the past few years we have introduced a greater variety of music in the 11 am service and often enjoy instrumentalists and the piano playing as well as the organ.

David Beckett was much loved. Since his death in 2014, Phil Henderson and John Shaw have played the organ, and Mel and Liz Turner with David and Elizabeth Handscomb have encouraged the choir to rehearse and to cheerfully lead our singing.

Flowers in the Church

According to the Encyclopaedia Britannica, the earliest flower arranging goes back to 2500 BC in Egypt. It reached Europe in about 1000 AD, where it began to be popular in churches and monasteries. Today flowers are an integral part of church life and worship, and contribute greatly to the beauty and dignity of regular services and special occasions.

Maureen Cook, who has lived all her life in Radley, has been masterminding the flower arranging in Radley for the past 27 years.

'I began to get involved in the flowers in the Church when I was asked to do the flowers on the pillars because the lady responsible could no longer reach up. Later I was asked to do the Christmas flowers and then took over responsibility for organising the flower rota at Easter 1989 and have been doing it ever since.

I had worked at the Radley Road Nurseries and was used to working with flowers, but I never had any training in flower arranging. It was just something I picked up and which I love doing. We have flowers in the Church every Sunday with special displays at Easter, Harvest Festival, Christmas and other special occasions such as Confirmation. I also have done the flowers for a number of weddings over the years and for some baptisms.

Sadly the number of people on the flower rota has decreased over the years so, with a few exceptions, the duty falls to me. In a typical week I water the flowers left over from Sunday on the Monday; go up on Thursday to see what needs doing; and buy and arrange the flowers on the Friday, which takes almost all morning. I supply most of the foliage from my own garden, as these days the foliage costs more than the flowers to buy! It is quite demanding week after week, but I really enjoy doing it. I find when I am up there arranging flowers I get lost in what I am doing. It is very therapeutic.'

Work with children and young people

In years gone by the traditional way of helping children understand their faith was by means of the catechism – a series of questions and answers which children were expected to learn by rote. More recently Sunday Schools and Sunday Clubs have become the standard way of bringing the Christian faith to children.

Sunday Schools, sometimes in times past called Sabbath Schools, were first set up in the 1780s, initially with the intention of bringing education to children unable to attend normal weekday schools. One of the pioneers in this movement was Robert Raikes. He proposed, in an article in the *Gloucester Journal*, that these schools should teach youngsters reading, writing, cyphering (arithmetic) and knowledge of the Bible. By 1785 at a time when the total population of England was 6.5 million, a quarter of a million children were attending Sunday Schools. By the mid nineteenth century, Sunday School attendance was a near universal aspect of childhood.

The Education Act of 1870 took away the need for Sunday Schools to teach general education. Since then they have focused on helping children learn about their faith in an interesting and informal environment.

In a religious census return of 1862, the Revd Robert Gibbings (see Chapter 5) wrote that there had been a Sunday School associated with Radley Church since 1807. He stated that it was currently meeting in a separate building near the Church and that there were 40 scholars. There were three unpaid female teachers and one paid male teacher.

Sunday Club

Today St James holds a Sunday Club at the same time as the 11 am service. The children meet separately in the Church Room and come in for the last part of the service.

Ann Ewens, a head of department at Oxford Brookes University, is one of those currently helping run the Sunday Club.

'When we first came to Radley we had a small daughter who began to attend the Sunday Club. A little later I responded to a request from the vicar at the time to help in the Club myself and have done so now for about 20 years.

Our aim is to introduce the children to the Christian faith in a friendly and non-judgmental environment. We teach the basics of the faith, including stories from the Bible. We have games, craft work and prayers. Drinks and biscuits/cake are provided. We meet for about 50 minutes and then join the congregation for the last part of the service and a blessing for the children at the communion table.

We have a team of six and each time have a leader, who prepares the material, and a helper. I am one of those who lead and I also organise the rota. Some of the older children (from the Young People's group) also help with the Sunday Club.

Numbers attending go up and down. In my time they have varied between six and 25. The Sunday Club is open to anyone, but the children attending are usually those of parents who come to the Church. In this, things are different from a generation or two ago. Then it was common for many children in the village to be sent to Sunday School whether their parents were churchgoers or not.

Our big event of the year is the Nativity Play, performed in the Church during the 11 am service on one of the Sundays shortly before Christmas. This takes much time to prepare and we begin early in November. It is very popular. The children love it and it brings in proud parents, families and friends.

Looking back over 20 years I can see how valuable the work of the Sunday Club has been. It has grounded many children in the faith – work which is continued as they move up to the Young People's group. Many have gone on to be part of the backbone of the Church. It also allows parents to go to the main service in the Church, knowing that their children are being well looked after.

There are challenges. We would love to see more children from non-regular churchgoers coming, as used to be the case. Also these days many activities now take place on Sundays, clashing with when we meet and families are often away at weekends. Nevertheless, I am convinced of the Sunday Club's importance. I find my involvement very rewarding, especially seeing children go on later to become mature Christians.'

The children in the Sunday Club were asked what the Church meant to them:

'It's like a family. It feels like a family.'

'You come and people say 'hello' and you say 'hello' back.'

'It is a place where you can be forgiven.'

'It is a place where you can have a relationship with God.'

'It is a good place to see friends even if you are not at the same school.'

'It is where people get married and come to at Christmas.'

They were also asked what they liked about the Church:

'It is good that it feels like a family.'

'We like the food.'

'We like the fact that we all share with each other.'

'You never really get seriously into trouble at church.'

'It is pretty and old and ornate with detail.'

'We like the people.'

'I would miss God if I didn't come to church.'

'We like the singing and music.'

Young People (YPs)

Sunday Club is for children up to 11 years old. Recently, work with older children, called Young People or YPs, has begun. Joanna Birkett, a physiotherapist by training, runs the YPs with two helpers.

'I had been involved in youth work in a previous church and soon after I moved to St James, a colleague and I became concerned for teenagers who had left the choir or finished with the Sunday Club and who were leaving the Church. We decided to try to provide something for those in this age group.

After experimenting with different material for a while we settled on that from 'Urban Saints'.[2] Initially we met during the main 11 am service, but now find it more appropriate to meet on Sunday evenings twice a month. On the fifth Sunday we have a lunchtime get together. We meet in my house because I feel a home environment is important. We play games and discuss a topic with a Christian or Biblical emphasis.

---

[2] A Christian children and youth organisation

At the moment we have about a dozen YPs aged between 11 and 18. The YPs also help with the Sunday Club and with the annual Kids' Club held during three days in the summer holidays. A recent important venture has been the building of the Hut by the Church Room for the use of children both from the Church and Radley Primary School, a Church of England school, including the YPs.

I enjoy young people, including playing silly games in their company. Above all I think it is very worthwhile work. It is important that youngsters know more about Christian life through sharing in discussion rather than just being taught. We aim to help them prepare for adulthood and give them a solid foundation of faith.

I am also involved in a very new project called 'Open the Book'. This recent nationwide venture takes us into the three schools in our benefice (Radley, Sunningwell, and Kennington). The aim is to present Bible stories through narration and through acting them out. We do this for the whole school, lasting about 15 minutes and finishing with a prayer. We stick firmly to the script given us because Open the Book is tailored to the school curriculum.

We have three teams of about five or six, each one with a leader. I am not one of the leaders. Each team goes to all three schools in one day. This takes place once a fortnight so each team is involved once every six weeks.

It is a very successful project, bringing an understanding of the Bible stories in a very relaxed and informal way. The children love it and so do the staff.'

The Church and the School

Radley Primary School and Radley Church have a close and good relationship. The children of the school are familiar with the Church building, both in terms of its facets and as a place of worship. Cohorts of children come into the Church and discover what the different features and areas mean, as well as looking at the props and colours used in worship. We discuss and even enact weddings and baptisms. Leavers' services, end of term, Christmas and Easter services are held here and it is a privilege and at times very moving to see the children themselves lead and take part in their worship.

Each year, a group of children from Year 4 spend an afternoon each week for a term discovering Godly Play – a reflective activity where they are able to wonder about and share some of the stories of God's people.

Godly Play

This contrasts well with Open the Book, when a team of adults from the benefice joins each fortnight in an assembly, enacting a story from *The Lion Storyteller Bible*, in costume, with audience participation. Often it is fun; sometimes it is profound.

The School helps us, too, by generously lending its hall for special occasions like refreshments after confirmation, and letting us use its playing field for our Kids' Club in the summer holidays and games for the YPs.

What the Church means to its adult members

Two of the older members of the Church were also asked what it meant to them.

Ann Blake, a physiotherapist by profession, has lived in Lower Radley since the 1960s.

'I had been a churchgoer in my youth but had rather let things slip. David Beckett, the organist and choirmaster, came to visit me in the early 1970s regarding a stewardship campaign for the Church. This was the nudge I needed and I began to attend St James and have done so ever since. I have been involved in many activities over the years. Early on I helped run the Church youth group for those aged 11 and older. I have attended a Home Group for some years and have helped with the Church flowers for even longer. I am a member of a Prayer Triplet, the Women's Fellowship and the Prayer Shawl Group. I also help to edit the monthly *Radley News*.

The Church means a great deal to me. I find a real warmth and friendship there and enjoy being with those who share the same outlook and values. The Home Group is especially important. The members know each other well and we can share concerns and issues with each other and support one another in prayer. There have been a number of vicars and clergy down the years and I have received much support and friendship from them.

The Church has played a major role in the growth of my faith. The Home Group in particular has helped my faith to be more meaningful and enabled me to understand spiritual matters more clearly. Without the Church and the faith that it encourages, my life would be a lot less fulfilled. In fact, there would be a large void. I am also convinced that many in the village who are not regular churchgoers would also miss the Church if it was not there. It means a lot to many, as witnessed by the response to the death watch beetle and bells appeals.'

Tom Garrud was a newspaper manager by profession following his service in the Royal Navy towards the end of the Second World War.

'I moved to Radley in 1985 and began attending St James then. I was sacristan, preparing for communion services, for a while and have attended a Home Group for many years. I was also Deanery Lay Chair for some years.

I love our Church. I feel a wonderful sense of belonging when I come to its services and enjoy being with a group of friends who have a common purpose. There is a great acceptance of one another. I find the variety of services very helpful and enjoy seeing people relate to and enjoy the more informal ones. The talks at the Reflect@6 evenings are always very good.

The Home Group is also very helpful and those there feel like my brothers and sisters, with a great care for each other. It is good to be able to air one's doubts in an accepting atmosphere.

I have been to many churches over the years, but my years in Radley have been ones where I have felt very comfortable and in tune with what takes place. St James is an essential part of my life. I find myself smiling as I enter the Church on Sundays, both outwardly and inwardly. I always experience the presence of God in the services.'

In addition three of the parents of YPs had the following to say about the Church:

'As a family we enjoy the Sunday worship and also the evening services. The Church means a lot as it has been our refuge many times in our life when we have faced difficulties. We have enjoyed seeing our children baptised, confirmed and married in our church! Like farming, the Church runs to the seasons and we are blessed to have such wonderful people attending to us throughout the year. Revd Pam has been amazing and an inspiration. We love the wooden pews and seats, and the warmth and atmosphere of God's house.'

'One of the reasons I love worshipping in St James Church is the sense of history all around me. As a history teacher I often picture past generations at prayer here and I get a real buzz looking up at the Henry VII stained glass window, the pulpit canopy from the House of Commons and imagining the villagers seeking refuge here during the Civil War. It is comforting to feel we are part of this continuing church story.'

'The Church at Radley has been an excellent way for me of getting closer to God on a slow journey, but it has also meant I have been able to bring my family along with this journey, and I think it will be for life and the next generation. The mix of worship, friendship and fun has meant there has been a way of keeping us all engaged.'

Sources

Interviews with Helen Beckett, Joanna Birkett, Ann Blake, Maureen Cook, Ann Ewens, Tom Garrud, David Handscomb, Yvonne Milward, Emma Moore, Katie North, Daphne Pollard, Sue Sowden, Iain Winton, Martha Young and other members of Radley Church

Christianity Today, August 2008

Encyclopaedia Britannica

'History of Sunday School', in *Towns' Sunday School Encyclopedia: A practical guide for Sunday School workers*, Elmer L. Towns, 1993

Photographs courtesy of Pam McKellen

Appendix 1: Timeline of Radley Church

The era of Abingdon Abbey

During this period, the church and village of Radley were effectively under the control of Abingdon Abbey. The Abbey built and replaced the church, were lords of the Manor, and received tithes and labour services from those who worked the land.

c.1000-1200	Radley's first Church built – date uncertain.
1271	First documentary evidence of Radley having a 'church', at the time a chapel of St Helen's Abingdon, which appointed a chaplain. Also first evidence of the chaplain having a house in Radley tied to his office.
c.1280	The church was destroyed by fire.
c.1295	Present church (probably just the chancel) built and consecrated.
c.1300	Present vicarage built.
1400-1500	Nave and tower added to church. Chancel largely rebuilt.
1538	Dissolution of Abingdon Abbey.

An independent parish

With the dissolution of Abingdon Abbey, Radley now had its own lord of the Manor living in the village and he soon acquired the right to appoint the vicar. This was a period of greater local assertiveness.

1544	First Radley incumbent, J. Standish, to be known by name.
1560	Purchase of Radley Manor by the Stonhouse family, who build a home in Radley Park.
1599	Register of baptisms, burials and marriages starts.
c.1600	Stonhouse family acquires the right to appoint Radley's vicar – the link with St Helen's becoming a formality only.
c.1622-1668	John Herbert is vicar, one of the longest serving and the first whose life we know much about.
1642-1646	Civil War and disease. Royalist officers and soldiers buried in churchyard. North aisle and transept reputedly destroyed.
c.1703	Church roof rebuilt by H. Perrin.
1720s	Stonhouses build new mansion in Radley Park.
1754	Five new church bells cast by Abel Rudhall of Gloucester.
1795	Bowyer family succeeds to the lordship of the Manor, with the right to appoint the vicar.
1801	West 'singing gallery' constructed and soon afterwards pulled down.

Victorian and Edwardian influences

This period brought new influences, associated with high Anglicanism and the Oxford Movement. The church interior became more ornate. The Bishop of Oxford sought to reduce the parish's independence.

1807-1852	John Radcliffe is vicar, one of the longest serving. Reinstates Norman font in 1840.
1847	Radley College founded and becomes influential in the church's affairs.
1840s	Bowyer family donates stained glass by Willement and continental choir stalls.
1868-1893	Radley College purchases the right to appoint the vicar and appoints three of its wardens (headmasters) in succession to the role.
1869	Extension to vicarage built with connecting corridor.
1877	Church porch built.
1893-1894	Charles Gore (later Bishop of Birmingham) is vicar. He is the first to be instituted by Bishop of Oxford. Brings his Community of the Resurrection to the vicarage.
1897	Bowyer family donates land to east of the church.
1902	Major restoration of church by C. Oldrid Scott.
1903	Organ installed in memory of Edwin Monk.
1910	Reredos in Oxford Movement style installed.

Adapting to a changing world

After the First World War, the village grew faster but the church could rely less on its patron and on traditional habits of attendance, and needed to win its congregation and finance. Buildings were modernised and made more flexible. Merger with other parishes helped ensure viability.

1937	Electric lighting installed in the church.
1963	Balcony at west end of nave constructed.
1983	Church Room built.
1989-1890	Major restoration of vicarage, now just the medieval building with the link to the Victorian building removed.
1990	United Benefice of Radley and Sunningwell created.
2004-2016	Pam McKellen is Radley's first female vicar.
2008-2009	Restoration of church following the death watch beetle infestation. The nave is reordered to allow much more flexible use.
2015	United Benefice extended to include Kennington.
2016	Bells rehung following major 'rapid fire' fundraising.

Appendix 2: Stonhouse and Bowyer family tree

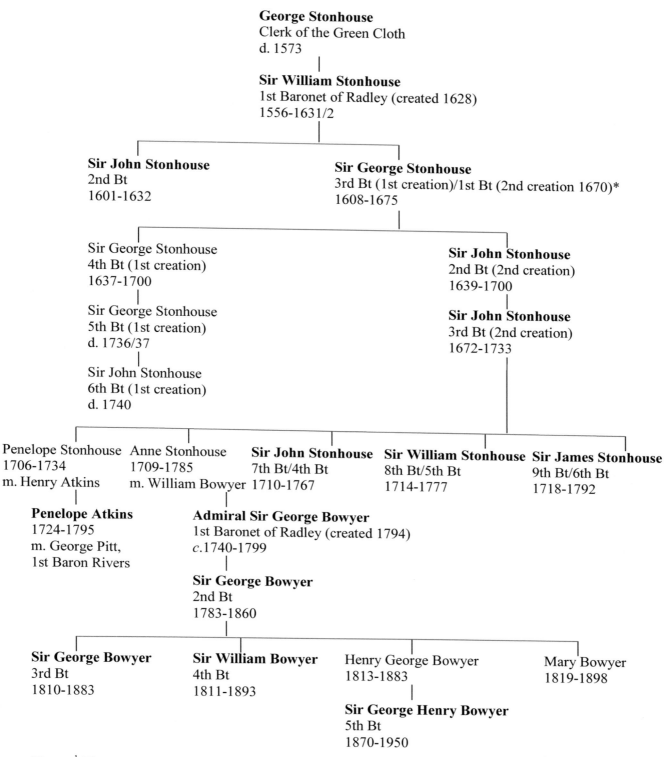

George Stonhouse
Clerk of the Green Cloth
d. 1573

Sir William Stonhouse
1st Baronet of Radley (created 1628)
1556-1631/2

Sir John Stonhouse
2nd Bt
1601-1632

Sir George Stonhouse
3rd Bt (1st creation)/1st Bt (2nd creation 1670)*
1608-1675

Sir George Stonhouse
4th Bt (1st creation)
1637-1700

Sir John Stonhouse
2nd Bt (2nd creation)
1639-1700

Sir George Stonhouse
5th Bt (1st creation)
d. 1736/37

Sir John Stonhouse
3rd Bt (2nd creation)
1672-1733

Sir John Stonhouse
6th Bt (1st creation)
d. 1740

Penelope Stonhouse
1706-1734
m. Henry Atkins

Anne Stonhouse
1709-1785
m. William Bowyer

Sir John Stonhouse
7th Bt/4th Bt
1710-1767

Sir William Stonhouse
8th Bt/5th Bt
1714-1777

Sir James Stonhouse
9th Bt/6th Bt
1718-1792

Penelope Atkins
1724-1795
m. George Pitt,
1st Baron Rivers

Admiral Sir George Bowyer
1st Baronet of Radley (created 1794)
*c.*1740-1799

Sir George Bowyer
2nd Bt
1783-1860

Sir George Bowyer
3rd Bt
1810-1883

Sir William Bowyer
4th Bt
1811-1893

Henry George Bowyer
1813-1883

Mary Bowyer
1819-1898

Sir George Henry Bowyer
5th Bt
1870-1950

Notes: [1] The accuracy of the dates from the sixteenth to eighteenth centuries cannot be guaranteed.
[2] The lords of Radley Manor are shown in bold. See Chapter 1 for details. The lords of the Manor acquired the right to appoint the vicar of Radley (the 'advowson') *c.*1600 and more generally acted as patrons of Radley Church. They continued to hold the advowson until 1867, when Sir George Bowyer sold it to the trustees of Radley College.
* Chapter 1 explains why there were two creations (1628 and 1670) of the Stonhouse baronetcy.

Appendix 3: List of incumbents from the mid sixteenth century

The list below follows the definition of 'incumbent' given on page 90 of Chapter 5. It includes all those appointed to serve as vicar of Radley, but not curates who assisted the vicar. For the period before Radley had its own vicar, the list includes chaplains appointed by the vicar of St Helen's Abingdon to serve Radley.

*c.*1544	J. Standish
*c.*1550	William Cross
*c.*1551-1553	Sir John Gibbons
*c.*1554-1556	Robert Francys
c.1558	Richard Cote
*c.*1568	Sir Randull Myllington
*c.*1586-1597	Richard Mansell
*c.*1602-1612/3	Roderick Lloyd
*c.*1612-1614	Roderick Jones
*c.*1615-1618	John Vaughan
*c.*1618-1625	Morgan Powell
*c.*1622-1668	John Herbert
1668-1680	William Carter
1681-1682	John Winchurst
1683-1698	John Stonhouse
1699-1709	Thomas Bayley (?)
1716-1745	Nathaniel Thompson
1754-1792	Sir James Stonhouse
1792-1796	John Bradford
1796-1800	John Lemprière (?)
1801-1803	Thomas Fry
1803-1805	Edward Lewton
1806-1807	Kenneth McKenzie Reid Tarpley
1807-1852	John Radcliffe
1852	William Beadon Heathcote
1853-1865	Robert Gibbings
1865-1867	William Henry Ranken
1868-1870	William Wood
1871-1879	Charles Martin
1880-1893	Robert James Wilson

1893-1894	Charles Gore
1895-1898	James Okey Nash
1898-1916	Charles Boxall Longland
1916-1921	Charles Stanley Phillips
1922-1925	Edward Heseltine Hibbert
1925-1928	Thomas Hearne Liddiard
1929-1936	Arthur Aubert Jackson
1936-1939	Francis Daly Briscoe
1939-1941	Eustace Edward Arthur Heriz-Smith
1941-1957	John Vincent Pixell
1957-1965	Robert Springett Brutton
1966-1971	Sydney Ernest Allso
1971-1988	Daniel Legh Pope
1988-1995	Keith Kinnaird
1996-2004	Thomas Patrick Gibbons
2004-2016	Pamela Joyce McKellen

Index

See also the *Timeline of Radley Church* on page 169 and the *List of Incumbents from the mid sixteenth century* on pages 172-173.